OTHER RANDOM HOUSE LAW MANUALS

Using a Lawyer
. . . And What to Do If Things Go Wrong
A Step-by-Step Guide

Small Claims Court
Making Your Way Through the System
A Step-by-Step Guide

Probate
How to Settle an Estate
A Step-by-Step Guide

Real Estate
The Legal Side to Buying a House, Condo, or Co-op
A Step-by-Step Guide

EVERYDAY CONTRACTS
Protecting Your Rights
A STEP-BY-STEP GUIDE

A RANDOM HOUSE PRACTICAL LAW MANUAL

EVERYDAY CONTRACTS
Protecting Your Rights
A STEP-BY-STEP GUIDE

**GEORGE MILKO,
KAY OSTBERG
& THERESA MEEHAN RUDY**
in Association with HALT

RANDOM HOUSE NEW YORK

HALT—An Organization of Americans for Legal Reform, is a national, nonprofit, nonpartisan, public-interest group with more than 150,000 members. Located at 1319 F. St. NW, Suite 300, Washington, DC 20004, its goals are to enable people to handle their legal affairs simply, affordably, and equitably. HALT's education and advocacy programs strive to improve the quality, reduce the cost, and increase the accessibility of the civil justice system. Its activities are funded by members' contributions.

Contributing authors: Katherine Lee and Allison Rottmann. Substantial assistance with this book was provided by Richard Hébert.

Library of Congress Cataloging-in-Publication Data
Milko, George.
Everyday contracts : protecting your rights : a step-by-step guide / by George Milko, Kay Ostberg & Theresa Rudy in association
with
HALT.
p.   cm.—(A Random House practical law manual)
Rev. ed. of: Everyday contracts / authors, Theresa Meehan, George Milko, Kay Ostberg.
Includes bibliographical references.
ISBN 0-679-73058-3
1. Contracts—United States—Popular works. I. Ostberg, Kay.
II. Rudy, Theresa.   III. HALT, Inc.   IV. Title.   V. Series.
KF801.Z9M55   1991   346.73'02—dc20   90-40957
[347.3062]

Book design by Charlotte Staub

Manufactured in the United States of America
Revised edition

Contents

Introduction

Though we may not be aware of it, most of us frequently enter into contracts in our daily lives . . . with the bank, a home-improvement contractor, a landlord, an auto-repair shop.

We don't think about reviewing such arrangements with a lawyer or even about carefully reading the fine print, partly because it doesn't seem to be worth the trouble, partly because we reason that such people are unlikely to change the terms of their standard agreements anyhow, even if we do take the time or spend the money on a lawyer.

But what if something goes wrong? It is then that the contract language becomes all-important. You may learn to your surprise that you have agreed to *accelerate* your loan payments, or that the bathroom repairs won't be completed until three months after your son's wedding.

Everyday Contracts tells you what to watch for before signing an agreement or verbally committing yourself to one. It explains what laws apply and translates the "boiler-plate" used in standard contracts into plain language. It provides important tips on how to read a contract, how to negotiate the best deal, and how best to get it in writing. Finally, the book tells you what your rights are if you have a dispute over a contract and where you can turn for help.

A WORD ABOUT TERMS

This book, unlike other HALT material, is full of legal terms. That is because they are used in contracts and it is our goal to translate them for you into understandable language. The book also explains the "fine print" so you can understand the contracts in your life without heading to a lawyer or a law library. Each legal term is italicized and defined the first time it is used. You can also consult the Glossary on page 247, where major terms and their definitions appear again.

HOW TO USE THIS BOOK

The first four chapters give basic information about all contracts. Chapters 1 and 2 explain basic contract language and laws, Chapter 3 gives basic consumer tips, and Chapter 4 explains avenues for resolving problems. After reading these, turn to the part that covers the agreement you're interested in.

Each part is devoted to one kind of contract or a "family" of contracts, with an explanation of the laws involved, tips about entering into the agreement, and a translation of standard contract terms into plain language. As appropriate, consumer-oriented provisions are suggested. Keep in mind, this is sample language; read it carefully before using it to be sure it's appropriate for the agreement you want.

Also listed are books, organizations, and dispute-resolution resources available if you need more help. Other resources are listed in the Bibliography, Appendix VI.

CONTRACT LAWS

It is often said that the basic right to make a deal, even a bad one, is found in the U.S. Constitution, and that we live in a "buyer beware" society. In fact, many laws do regulate our contracts. These range from "common law" principles, derived by our courts from early English precedents, to state laws that govern the buying and selling of goods and services, most of them variations of what's known as the Uniform Commercial Code. Several federal agencies, notably the Federal Trade Commission, the Federal Reserve Board, and the U.S. Department of Housing and Urban Development, also enforce laws that regulate contracts. These often also have state counterparts.

Knowing about these laws and agencies can make the difference between being taken advantage of and making good agreements with which you can live comfortably.

PROFESSIONAL HELP

Everyday Contracts gives you information you need to feel confident preparing, negotiating, and signing a contract on your own, without professional legal help. Going it alone may be your only option if you need your car repaired today, are handed a lease to sign in a city with a housing crisis, or are getting a loan from the only bank in town. However, if possible, when considerable money is at stake or you are uncertain about a substantial part of the deal, consider hiring professional help. *But before you hire anyone, know your options.*

Decide, first, whether you want someone to help you negotiate the contract, draft it, or review an agreement that's already written. The more you want done, the higher the fee will be.

Investigate all your alternatives. You may not need a lawyer. Instead, a competent paralegal, experienced nonlawyer, or a consumer group may be able to help, particularly if you simply want someone to review a standard agreement. Whomever you hire, negotiate a fair fee. Ask others what they charge. A lawyer will probably quote an hourly fee, but you can try to negotiate a flat fee or an hourly fee with an agreed-upon maximum.

Be clear whether you want help in negotiating the contract or only a review of the agreement you're planning to sign. If you ask only for a review and can specify which clauses you want help with, it will keep your cost down. Whatever you agree on, remember: That's a contract, too. Get it in writing, including the work that will be done, when it will be done, how much you'll pay, and when you'll pay it.*

*See *Using a Lawyer,* Kay Ostberg in association with HALT, Random House, 1990.

PART I

CONTRACTS IN GENERAL

CHAPTER 1

THE CONTRACT

Julie's car makes funny noises. She takes it to her neighborhood repair shop. A service representative estimates the job will cost $350. She leaves the car and arranges to pick it up at the end of the day.

Bill has finally agreed to sell Jim his stereo. Jim agrees to pay Bill $300 for it next payday.

Beth's mom agrees to let her live at home rent free for the rest of her life if Beth will take care of her when her health declines.

Mary's landlord doesn't want to renew her lease but says she can live in the house month-to-month on the same terms as in her previous lease. Mary agrees.

Andrew receives a mailed invitation to join a prepaid legal services plan before September 3. He signs the registration form and sends it on September 2.

In each of these examples, chances are a legally binding, valid contract* has been entered into. A contract is any agreement between two or more people. It involves a "meeting of the minds" expressed orally or in writing to do or not do something in exchange for something else.

It is a popular misconception that a contract must be signed or notarized to be valid or that you must pay at least

---

*In this book, the terms *contract, agreement,* and *deal* are used interchangeably.

one dollar to make a deal "stick." People even think that a contract must be in writing.

Although it's true some contracts must be in writing (explained later in this chapter), for the most part oral contracts are legal. However, although legal, they aren't usually smart. HALT strongly urges that you get any agreement in writing to protect against misunderstandings and later problems.

The underlying principle of the marketplace, still the cornerstone of contract law, is that once a bargain is made, it should be upheld. This promotes predictability and protects everyone's right to make a deal. As a result, judges still try hard to uphold any deal. In some instances, courts will uphold a contract even if it means filling in terms of the deal that were left out or vague. They will use tradition or what is customary in the business or industry to supply the missing information.

In recent decades, laws have been enacted to protect consumers' contract rights, a recognition that businesses and consumers often have unequal bargaining power. However, courts still rely on the basic principle that a contract should be upheld whether or not it reflects a fair bargain.

With this in mind, you have a valid contract if you have:

- An offer, counteroffer, and acceptance
- Consideration
- Itemized terms
- No valid defenses

OFFER AND ACCEPTANCE

An offer is an invitation to make a deal or an invitation to exchange promises. An offer might be someone stopping you on the street and telling you, "For only $10, you can be the proud owner of this genuine cut-glass fake ruby ring." Or it can be a newspaper advertisement promising a television set at the sale price of $400 to the first 10 buyers.

You can tell when an offer is made because all that's needed to clinch the agreement is your acceptance, signaled by your agreeing to the deal on the terms offered. This can be by oral acceptance, signing on the proverbial "dotted line," or, in the example of the ring, handing over $10 to the fellow on the street. Watch out for jokes, though. If it was not reasonable to believe an offer was really made, you have no contract.

Beware of something else, too. Sometimes all it takes for acceptance is your silence. Record and book clubs, for example, get you to "agree" that if they don't hear from you after notifying you of each month's selection, you have "accepted" the offer to buy that selection at the listed price.

In other cases, you accept by completing your side of the agreement (called *performance*). For example, your brother says, "If you paint the outside of my house this summer, I'll pay you $1,500 plus the cost of supplies." All you need to do to accept the arrangement is start painting the house.

An acceptance isn't a *counteroffer*. If you say, "Sure, I'll take that dynamite ring, but I'll only give you $7 for it," you've made a counteroffer, not an acceptance. A counteroffer is considered to cancel the original offer. No contract exists unless the counteroffer is accepted. Not only is the ring seller not obligated to sell you the ring for $7, once you've made your counteroffer, the seller is not even obligated to sell it to you for $10.

You also can withdraw an offer anytime before it is accepted. So, if the ring seller says, "Oops, I changed my mind. I don't want to sell you this fine ring," and you have not yet agreed to buy it or whipped out your $10, the offer is rescinded, and you have no right to buy the ring. (Some states make exceptions and prohibit businesses to rescind offers they have promised in writing to keep open for a specified time.)

Similarly, you have only a reasonable amount of time in which to accept an offer. Although what is considered a reasonable time varies, it's safe to say that if you accept an offer years after it was made, even though it was never formally rescinded, it's unlikely a contract was created by your acceptance.

CONSIDERATION

To have a valid contract, there must also be an exchange. Each side must give up something, called *consideration.* Consideration is the glue that binds a deal; it answers the question "What do I get out of it?" The most common consideration is money for goods or services, as in the sale of the ring. In that deal, one side gave up the ring and the other gave up the cash.

Consideration can also be a promise to do or not do something. In one of the examples at the beginning of this chapter, the consideration was a promise to care for an ill parent in return for free rent. Other forms of nonmonetary consideration might be a promise not to sue, or a promise to hold open an offer to sell property.

However, if your best friend says, "I'll take you to Paris if I win the lottery," and you agree, no contract exists because no exchange of consideration has taken place. You have not given up anything.

Also, if you agree to something you already previously agreed to or are already legally bound by, there is no consideration and therefore no contract. For example, if you call up a creditor and say, "I'll only pay you the $500 I owe you if you don't charge me the interest we had agreed upon," you are making an offer with no consideration. You already owe the money and the interest. Even if the creditor agrees, chances are you still legally owe the interest from the original deal.

Finally, the law does not require that the consideration be "fair" for the contract to be binding. To do so is considered interfering with the right to bargain. (Exceptions to this "right to make a bad bargain" are discussed later in the chapter.)

TERMS

For a contract to be valid, it should also be clear who is making the contract and what property, time, place, price, and other pertinent details are involved. These material terms define each side's rights and obligations. Some states have laws that specifically address failure by a business to disclose the material terms of an agreement (see Chapter 5, Bank Loans).

If essential terms are missing or are so indefinite as to make the contract unclear, no "meeting of the minds" has occurred and, technically, no contract has been entered into. The contract is void. On the other hand, if many of the terms in a contested contract are clear, a court may try to fill in the missing or unclear terms with a "best guess" as to what both sides intended to agree on. A court will consider past usage in contracts of the industry or past contracts between both sides.

If the terms were mistakenly stated, the person who made the mistake can be held to it unless the mistake was obvious: for example, if a real ruby was offered and the quoted price was missing a few zeroes. If both sides made mistakes in defining the terms and either side wants to cancel the contract, the contract can be voided. (Please note the difference between *void* and *voidable.* If a contract is void, there is no contract. If a contract is voidable, there is a contract until one side or the other chooses to nullify it.)

DEFENSES

You have an offer, an acceptance, consideration, and clear terms, but you still do not have an enforceable contract if one side or the other has a valid defense against enforcing it. Be mindful, however, that basic public policy is to uphold contracts whenever possible, so it is usually stiff going to prove a defense.

Before explaining some valid defenses, it's worthwhile mentioning some that are not valid. A court will not let you out of a contract if you're challenging it because you:

- Failed to read the contract
- Changed your mind (see Chapter 3 for some exceptions)
- Can't pay
- Didn't have the agreement notarized

Valid defenses include: that a contract was entered into for illegal purposes; that one or both sides were not competent to enter into the contract; that the contract violates the state's Statute of Frauds; that one side was forced or tricked into signing; and that the contract includes "unconscionable" provisions. Each of these is discussed below.

Illegal Purpose

A contract with an illegal purpose is no contract at all. It's considered void. Thus, if you want to put terms in writing because you don't trust the arsonist you hired to burn down your financially failing business, don't bother. You won't create a contract, only evidence of your crime.

However, if, for example, you sign a loan agreement that obligates you to pay an illegally high interest rate (usury), a court might reduce the interest rate to the highest legal level before enforcing the contract. Although the consideration was illegal, the purpose of the contract was not, and the court will make its best effort to uphold the bargain. (This is called *reformation*).

Incompetence to Contract

The law identifies certain people as lacking the capacity to enter into a valid contract. They include minors (usually under age 18), the mentally unstable, and people who enter into an agreement while under the influence of drugs or alcohol. An incompetent person or that person's legal caretaker *(guardian)* has the right to cancel a contract, but a court will also try to correct any injustice the cancellation creates. If a parent cancels a child's purchase agreement for a stereo, for example, chances are good that a court will order the stereo returned to its previous owner.

A word of caution, however, to anyone planning to use the drug-and-alcohol defense: courts are reluctant to allow anyone to cancel a contract based on the defense of incapacitating intoxication. To plead this defense successfully, you'll need to show that when the deal was clinched, the other side knew about your intoxication and took advantage of you.

Statute of Frauds

Some contracts must be in writing. These are listed in each state's Statute of Frauds and Uniform Commercial Code. Although state laws differ, the most common contracts that must be in writing are for the sale of goods worth more than $500, the sale of land, the sale of securities, auto repairs, sales warranties, and consumer loans. Also, contracts that won't be fulfilled within one year must be in writing.

If you have one of these contracts and it's not in writing, either you or the other side may cancel it. Be mindful, however, that some courts may enforce an oral agreement if one side relied on the promises of the other and put up money or some other significant investment.

Fraud, Duress, and Undue Influence

A contract is voidable if you were forced or tricked into signing it, threatened with serious harm, or, while you were in a weakened condition, strongly pressured by someone in a financial or confidential relationship with you. Those considered to be in a financial or confidential relationship include your doctors, lawyers, accountants, clergy, and members of your family. Courts are reluctant to accept this defense, but if a gun was held to your head, or if you clearly were taken advantage of by someone close to you while you were ill, or if one side of the bargain was clearly misrepresented, most courts will hold the contract void.

Unconscionable Provisions

This defense is relatively new. It has been used successfully when the two people who made the deal have unequal bargaining power. Anyone subject to an unreasonable clause in a contract can ask the court to cancel that clause or, sometimes, even the entire deal. This defense has been allowed to protect people from having to live with one-sided "take it or leave it" contracts. However, terms that are considered "unconscionable" are usually defined by court precedents.

Some unconscionable provisions are: a clause in a hospital emergency admission form that waives all claims for medical malpractice against the hospital or doctors, and a clause that allows a retail store to take back *all* merchandise bought on credit even though most of it has been paid for. In such instances, a court may strike the unconscionable clause but uphold the rest of the contract.

Having a valid contract is no guarantee that problems won't develop, however. The other side may not stick to the deal, or you may change your mind about what you thought was a great deal when you signed. The next chapter explains your rights when a contract dispute arises and what can happen if you decide to back out of a legally binding agreement.

CHAPTER 2

ENFORCEMENT

When someone fails to live up to the terms of a contract, it's called a *breach.* When that happens, you can negotiate, mediate, or sue for damages. Knowing what a court might award in such cases can help you negotiate a settlement directly, go into mediation with some understanding of your legal rights, or assess whether it's worth your time and money to sue. It also will help you write into your contract explicit protections against breach.

Common-law principles developed to govern buying and selling in the marketplace. The underlying marketplace principle is that the side that breached the contract should pay for the losses caused by the breach, but not be additionally penalized for breaking the contract. A punishment payment is not required.

In deciding whether a breach has occurred, if the contract can still be upheld, and what might be owed, a court will not deviate greatly from custom and tradition for a given business unless the terms of your contract clearly specify otherwise.

With this in mind, if a breach occurs, you may get one or more of the following remedies. Each of the remedies discussed in later chapters fits under one or another of these categories.

DAMAGES

The remedy most frequently awarded by a court is money to compensate for loss caused by the breach *(damages)*. For example, if you were one of the first ten buyers to arrive to pick up that television set for $400, as advertised, and you found all the sets already sold, the store "owes" you any amount above the $400 that you had to pay to buy the set somewhere else.

There are limits to what you can recover, however, even if you can show a loss. If your mother had a heart attack because she was worried when you didn't call her, you will probably not be able to recover her medical expenses from the telephone company by claiming it failed to hook up your service when promised.

You can get compensation only for losses that are a foreseeable result of the breach. In the example above, it is unlikely a court would find that the telephone company could have foreseen that connecting your telephone late would injure your mother. Damages are considered foreseeable if both sides know in advance that the damages are likely to occur because of the breach. You also need to keep in mind two other limits on damages.

Another limitation is that you have an obligation to try to avoid increasing the damages that result from a breach even though the other side caused the breach. If you have an opportunity to mitigate the damages and you don't, you may never recover for the loss.

Say your roofer failed to patch all the holes in your roof and your upstairs floor was ruined by a subsequent rain. You have a responsibility to mop up the water before it seeps through the ceiling and damages the floor below. If you don't, you may not be reimbursed for the damage to the lower floor.

Even if you write a clause into your contract setting out

how much money will be owed to you if the contract is broken, the amount must be sensible in light of the losses likely to occur. (Clauses that specify how much will be owed are called *liquidation* clauses.)

EXCUSED COUNTERPERFORMANCE

This is just a fancy way of saying that if the other side fails to live up to its side of a deal, you have no obligation to live up to yours: You are released from your part of the agreement. As a lawyer would say, you are excused from *performance.*

One caution, however: a court will not let you out of the contract if it finds that the breach was minor. So, if your brother agreed to pay you $1,200 for painting his house and you painted everything but the front porch, a court won't let your brother out of paying you. Chances are the court will instead award you the $1,200 minus reasonable costs to hire someone to finish the job.

QUASI-CONTRACT

Even if, in the housepainting example, your contract explicitly stated that your brother would pay you only if the painting was completed exactly as specified, the court will still probably order your brother to pay you something. However, instead of looking at the contract to determine how much you're owed, the court will calculate the fair market value of the work you did complete. This is called suing in quasi-contract. In other words, the court will award money based not on the written contract, but on the principle that your brother should not unfairly benefit from your work by not paying anything for it. When a contract results from unequal bargaining power or the outcome doesn't seem fair in light of typical business practices, a court may use this principle to reform a contract.

RESCISSION AND RESTITUTION

If one side breaks a contract by not coming up with money or other promised consideration, the court may allow the other side to cancel the contract and get back anything that has already been paid. This is called *rescission.* For example, if you learn that the "new" piano you bought was really used, the seller has failed to come up with the promised consideration. A court will probably let you return the piano for a refund. Of course, if you played the piano for a year before returning it, the court has two choices: It may deduct a rental fee from that refund or decide that since you didn't discover the misrepresentation for a year, it couldn't have been serious. In that case, it will consider you to have affirmed the contract by using the piano.

SPECIFIC PERFORMANCE

In rare instances, when a court doesn't think money can adequately repay you for a breach, it may order the other side to live up to the agreement. Courts will award such specific performance only if they think the contract was fair to start with and you can't replace the services reasonably elsewhere.

TORT ACTION

If a broken contract caused someone to be injured or property to be damaged (a *tort*), you may be able to sue for damages, but only if both sides could foresee that the breach might cause the injury. For example, you buy medication that's prepared incorrectly and as a result you suffer ill effects; a court will probably uphold your claim for damages from the manufacturer based on the misrepresentation and incorrect preparation of the medicine.

CHAPTER 3

BEFORE YOU SIGN

We suggest reading this chapter now and rereading it immediately before you enter into any contract. It contains practical suggestions about what to keep in mind when entering into an agreement.

PRACTICAL RULES

Get It in Writing.   Many oral contracts are legal, but unless you want to risk a courtroom contest over whose word is more believable, get the agreement in writing. Many, if not most, contract disputes result from misunderstanding the terms of the agreement. Putting the terms in writing usually helps both sides understand them clearly. Also, it's easier to hold the other side to the agreement if it's in writing and you can point to it if problems develop.

Don't Sign Anything Unless You're Sure.   Make sure you understand all the terms of an agreement before accepting it. Do not simply listen to a salesperson's description of the agreement; read it thoroughly. Although there may be instances when you have little choice but to sign immediately, you do this at some risk. Ask questions about language you don't understand. If you have doubts, ask to take the agreement home so you can go over it with someone you trust who has knowledge or experience in the subject area.

Change the Language to Fit the Terms. Make sure all the terms you are agreeing to are written into the contract. Don't let a salesperson tell you, "Oh, we never go by that clause, it's just standard language left over from before," or "The cost includes free delivery even though it's not listed in the agreement." Change the language to reflect the agreement. Whenever possible, cross out clauses that are incorrect, add new language, and have both signers initial in the margin next to each change.

Fill in the Blanks. Make sure all blank spaces in standard-form contracts are filled in or crossed out. Otherwise, they may be filled in later without your knowledge. Never sign a blank agreement.

Make Sure You Know the Payment Schedule. If the contract involves payments you'll owe, make sure you know the full amounts, all interest or other charges, when payments are due, and what happens if you fail to pay on time. Some state laws require banks and other lenders to give you a payment schedule if you ask for one. Always ask.

Keep a Copy of the Agreement. This is your evidence that a deal was made. Your copy should have original signatures, if at all possible. This is considered an "original." Keep the contract in a safe place.

Consider Adding a Mediation or Arbitration Clause. If you have a chance to change a contract or are drafting one, consider adding a provision that if problems arise that can't be solved directly, you will take them to either *mediation* or *arbitration*. These alternative dispute-resolution forums are quicker, less expensive, and less time-consuming than suing in court.

In mediation, you and the other side identify problems and discuss solutions with the guidance of a neutral mediator. Any agreement you make must be put into writing before it is legally binding. Once you sign the agreement, it has the legal force of any contract.

Arbitration is more formal than mediation. Rules of court do not apply; it is similar to a shortened, less formal court hearing. Each side submits a summary of its arguments to an arbitrator, who then makes a decision that is put in writing.

SPECIAL LAWS

When signing any agreement, you should also know about two other kinds of laws that govern consumer contracts: rules that require a "cooling-off" period for some contracts and plain-language requirements.

The Cooling-Off Rule

If you sign a contract other than at the seller's normal place of business, such as in your home, chances are you have three days to change your mind and cancel it. This rule is intended primarily to prevent door-to-door salespeople from pushing you into expensive, unplanned purchases. When you sign the contract, the seller is also obligated to give you a cancellation form to use if you change your mind and choose to exercise your rights under this rule.

This cooling-off rule is enforced by the Federal Trade Commission and applies to any contract that meets all of these requirements:

- It is not made at the seller's normal place of business.
- It is not made by telephone or mail.
- It is for more than $25.
- It is not for real estate, insurance, or securities.
- It is not for emergency home repairs.

Plain-Language Laws

Some states require that all consumer contracts be written in clear, coherent, and nontechnical language. Many more states apply this requirement to insurance contracts. In states that have such plain-language laws, you can sue a business if you can show that because you did not understand confusing or technical language, you suffered a monetary or other loss. Contact your state or local Consumer Protection Agency (Appendix I) for further information about your state's plain-language laws.

CHAPTER 4

SOLVING PROBLEMS

If you have a problem with your contract—either before or after you sign—review this chapter as well as the problem-solving tips and resources in the chapters that discuss your subject area.

If you're having a contract problem, you have several standard options for solving it, no matter what kind of contract it is:

- Direct negotiation with the other side
- Filing a complaint with a government or private consumer agency
- Participating in arbitration or mediation
- Taking your complaint to court

DIRECT NEGOTIATION

When you suspect you have a problem with your landlord, your home-improvement contractor, your bank, or someone else you have a contract with, try to sort it out first by direct contact. This is not only the least expensive option, it also lets you clear up problems that are simply misunderstandings.

Check your contract before you call or write. If you call, regardless of the outcome of your conversation, put your concerns in a letter to the other party to document the problem and any agreement you reached. This creates a "paper trail" that may be useful if you later have to take your complaint to arbitration.

If you can't solve the problem by talking to the other person involved, try that person's supervisor or the Consumer Affairs or Customer Relations Office of the business you've contracted with, if it has one. If it is a large company you are complaining to, it may have a toll-free "800" number you can use.

LOCAL AND STATE AGENCIES

If direct negotiation fails, try taking your complaint to a government or private agency. These typically offer help in resolving consumer problems at little or no expense. For almost all consumer complaints, you can get help from either a government-run Consumer Affairs Office or the privately operated Better Business Bureau (see Private Agencies, below). In some cases, you might want to contact a trade association or media-sponsored consumer "action line."

City and county Consumer Protection Agencies often act as neutral intermediaries to help resolve complaints. This can be effective because these agencies' staffs are usually familiar with the business practices and relevant laws in your area. The agencies typically limit the type of complaints they handle, however. For example, they do not usually handle landlord-tenant problems or problems with service professionals, such as lawyers.

If your city or county doesn't have a Consumer Protection Agency, contact your state agency (Appendix I). It will operate either as a separate Department of Consumer Affairs or as part of the office of the governor or attorney general. If the office nearest you doesn't handle your type of problem, it should be able to refer you to one that does.

Consumer Protection Agencies have authority to force businesses to respond to your complaint, and can even sue businesses on your behalf. However, because their resources are limited, they usually sue only businesses with serious patterns of illegal activity.

Filing a complaint with a government-run Consumer Protection Agency may lead in either direction—to a mediated resolution or to a bureaucratic shuffle that offers you little more than advice on whether or not you have a valid legal claim. To find out what you can expect from your agency, call and ask how they handle individual complaints.

U.S. GOVERNMENT AGENCIES

Although almost every area of consumer concern is the responsibility of one federal agency or another, these agencies usually work on overall regulation, such as by promulgating "Truth in Lending" rules, not on individual complaints. It's worthwhile, however, to ask the agency that deals with your area of concern what consumer information it has available and if it is one of the few that does investigate complaints.

PRIVATE AGENCIES

Better Business Bureaus (BBBs) are nonprofit, private organizations sponsored by local businesses. Currently, there are 170 BBB offices in the United States. (Their addresses are listed in Appendix II.) Besides compiling complaint records on local businesses, they usually try to resolve consumers' problems through direct negotiation with the business. Some also offer binding arbitration.

About 40,000 trade and professional organizations in the United States represent the interests of banks, insurers, medicine, other professional services, and every major industry and manufacturing group. Some trade associations run their own mediation or arbitration programs either directly or through a service council or consumer action program. If you decide to use one of these, make sure you know exactly what you are agreeing to and try to find out whether it has a reputation for fairness or bias toward the businesses it represents.

Many local radio and television stations and newspapers also sponsor consumer-mediation programs, typically called "action lines" or "hot lines." They use media exposure to pressure businesses into cooperating in dispute settlement. Some programs are selective in the complaints they take, reserving their resources for the "worst" cases. To learn what's available in your area, contact your local newspaper and radio or television stations.

The best way to register a complaint with any agency is by writing a letter. Include copies of your contract, bills, and any other documents relevant to the dispute. Remember to keep a copy for your files. Your letter should include:

- Your name, address, and telephone number where you can be reached both at home and at work
- The name and address of the business you are complaining about
- A *brief* description of the problem and supporting facts
- The amount of money involved, if any
- The resolution you want

ARBITRATION AND MEDIATION

If federal, state, county, city, or private Consumer Protection Agencies can't help resolve your dispute, investigate using a public or private arbitration or mediation service. These *alternative dispute-resolution forums* are often less expensive than going to court and, in the case of mediation, emphasize cooperative resolution rather than pitting adversaries against each other. This is particularly important if you know that you will have future dealings with the other side.

As explained earlier, in *mediation* you and the other side identify problems and discuss solutions with the guidance of a neutral mediator. Mediation is not for every dispute, however. If either side is hostile or unwilling to talk to the other, mediation may not work. Also, shop carefully for your mediator. This person can influence the process significantly. Any agreement you make must be put into writing before it is legally binding, at which time it has the legal force of any contract.

Shopping for a mediator is a little different from shopping for other service professionals because most mediators are not in private practice. Instead, most belong to a community group or court program. You'll probably end up interviewing the program administrator first and the particular mediator only later. When interviewing a mediator or program administrator, be sure to ask:

- Does the mediator specialize, for example, in consumer disputes?
- Where was the mediator trained?
- How long has the mediator been practicing?
- How many cases has the mediator handled? Were they similar to yours?
- How much will mediation cost? Are unforeseen increases in cost likely? Under what circumstances?

Arbitration is a more formal process than mediation. Although the rules of court do not apply, it is similar to a shortened, less formal court hearing. Each side submits a summary of its arguments to an arbitrator (or panel of arbitrators), who then makes a decision.

Before you agree to arbitrate, be sure you know whether the decision will be binding. If it is binding, the arbitrator's decision is enforceable in court. Although a binding process is final and therefore guarantees quick resolution, be sure you feel comfortable with the process, your arbitrator, and the people who run the program.

Ask your local courts if they run a mediation or arbitration program, and check the telephone directory for listings of private arbitrators or mediators. You might also contact the Society of Professionals in Dispute Resolution (SPIDR) or the American Bar Association Standing Committee on Dispute Resolution for more information and referrals. Both are located in Washington, D.C.

SUING IN COURT

If none of these alternatives works, consider suing. Keep in mind that this should be your last resort because of the expense, time, and frustration it usually entails. Before deciding to sue, carefully weigh the costs against your chances of winning and the amount you are likely to win.

If your dispute involves a small sum of money, you may be able to sue inexpensively in small claims court. This is far preferable to taking a claim to district or municipal court. Small claims courts offer a quick, informal, and fairly consumer-hospitable forum. Most do not take cases that involve more than $2,500, although the limits differ from state to state.* If your claim is for more than the small claims limit,

*For state limits, call your court or get a copy of *Small Claims Court,* Theresa Meehan Rudy in association with HALT, Random House, 1990. This step-by-step guide

consider filing suit in the next-highest court, usually municipal or district court, or sue for less so your claim can be handled in small claims court.

Taking a case through small claims court has many advantages over higher courts. The process is streamlined, you can represent yourself (in some states, lawyers aren't even allowed in the courtroom unless they're defending themselves), filing fees are lower, and you can usually get a hearing within 30 or 40 days.

If you represent yourself in a higher court, you'll be expected to know which court to file in, what the rules of procedure are, how to collect evidence, how to discern what evidence is and isn't admissible, when to file papers, what the different legal terms mean, and how to present your case to the judge. Also, don't be surprised by longer delays, higher filing fees, and a judge who isn't at all happy to see you there without a lawyer.

If you don't choose to represent yourself but decide to hire a lawyer to handle the suit, calculate how much you stand to win after deducting your lawyer's fees and expenses, including court fees.

---

will also explain how to file papers, collect evidence, present your case to the judge, and enforce an award in court.

PART II

TAKING
A LOAN

CHAPTER 5

BANK
LOANS

Sally and Suzanne decide to open an office-cleaning business. They have customers and staff, but they need money to buy equipment. They talk to three banks. Their best loan offer is $20,000 at 10% interest to be repaid at $424.94 a month for five years.

Alan's three credit cards are "maxed out." He owes $3,000 on the first, $2,000 on the second, $5,000 on the third, and pays 18% interest on each. He checks with his local bank and decides to pay off his accounts with a loan for $10,000 at 14% interest, to be repaid in 36 monthly payments of $341.78.

Ellen is buying a car for $9,000, and because sales are slow, the dealer offers financing at 2% with no money down payable in 36 monthly payments of $257.78. After three years, she will have paid $9,280.08 for this loan—$9,000 for the car, and $280.08 for the interest.

Loans like these are agreements to lend money (the *principal*) in exchange for a fee, called *interest,* usually based on a percentage of the loaned amount. Bank loans typically involve standard forms, government regulations, and collateral—the property you "put up" as security that you'll forfeit if you don't pay back the loan. Because most bank loans require collateral, they are considered *secured* loans.

GOVERNMENT REGULATION

Consumer loans are regulated by several government agencies. The Federal Reserve Board, the Federal Trade Commission, and state and federal banking authorities all have a role in regulating and monitoring consumer lending. In addition, these agencies enforce laws to make sure that people are not denied credit on illegal grounds.

The regulations are intended to protect consumers by seeing to it that they are aware of all the terms of the loan and their full financial obligations. The agencies' roles, the laws they enforce, and how you can get redress if those laws and regulations are violated are all discussed later in this and the next chapter. First, you will find an overview of basic loan concepts, followed by consumer problem-solving tips and resources. The final chapter in this section offers a clause-by-clause analysis of a typical bank-loan contract. Secured loans from nonbank lenders, like finance companies, car dealerships, and furniture stores, often include identical clauses.

BASIC CONCEPTS

Most people who borrow use *installment* loans. That means they repay the loan over time in monthly or other periodic payments. In *consideration* for the loan, they agree to repay the principal and the interest. The length of time they have to pay back a loan is called its *term*.

How Interest Rates Are Set
All banks get their money from Federal Reserve Banks, operated by the Federal Reserve Board. This board, appointed by the president of the United States, controls the flow of the nation's money supply. One of its most important tools for doing this is the *discount* rate of interest that it

charges its member banks for the money they borrow. The board sets that rate as a political and economic strategy to keep the economy healthy. Banks in turn base their rates on the discount rate, charging customers a little more than they themselves have to pay "the Fed."

The *prime rate* is the interest that the largest banks charge their preferred, or "prime," borrowers—typically huge corporations. All other interest rates are set higher than the prime, reflecting the banks' perception of their costs and the risks they take that the loans won't be repaid. Banks make consumer loans based on two types of interest rates: *fixed* and *fluctuating.*

Fixed-Rate Loans

A fixed-rate loan has the same interest rate applied throughout its life. Because fixed interest rates don't change, you can calculate before signing exactly what the loan will cost you each month and over its entire life.

Fluctuating-Rate Loans

The cost of a loan with a fluctuating interest rate varies over the life of the loan. The interest rate usually goes up or down with the prime rate, with a special rate set by the Office of Thrift Supervision for mortgages, or with the current interest being paid for U.S. Treasury bills, the money the U.S. government borrows.

Because fluctuating rates have many variations, you should call around and shop for the best deal. Things to look for when comparing fluctuating-rate loans include:

- How *often* your rate can be changed
- The limit on how many percentage points your rate can be adjusted at any one time (a *yearly* or *periodic* cap)
- The limit on how much your rate can be changed over the entire life of the loan (a *lifetime* cap)

For example, you might have a five-year loan for $5,000 at the prime rate plus 2%, with an annual adjustment, a 1% yearly cap and a lifetime cap of 3%. If the prime is at 10% at the start of the loan, your beginning interest rate will be 12%. At the first annual adjustment, that rate can go up to 13% or down to 11%. As the prime rate changes, so will your interest rate. However, your rate can go up only to 13% the first year, 14% the second, and 15% the third. The lifetime 3% cap means the highest rate you will ever have to pay on that loan is 15%. The cap also means the lowest interest rate you'll pay is 9%, the original 12% rate minus 3%, even if the prime goes below 7%. Some loans apply the cap to the maximum that can be charged but not to the minimum, a decided advantage for you if prevailing interest rates decline steadily or steeply.

Calculating Interest

Banks charge interest on the declining balance of the principal of your loan. At the start, the interest is assessed against the entire amount of the loan. A chunk of what you pay goes to interest, with only what's left over applied to reducing the principal. On your second payment, the interest is assessed on the entire amount of the original loan less that part of the first payment that was applied to lower the principal. Each time you make a payment, you reduce the principal more and thus also reduce the amount used to pay the interest. This is called *amortization.*

Say you take out a fixed loan of $13,000 for 9% interest payable over five years. Your first payment is $269.86. Banks divide each payment you make between principal and the interest. In this example, $172.36 of your first payment goes to pay off the principal and $97.50 ($13,000 times .09 annual interest divided by 12 months) goes to the interest (see box). At your second payment, the interest is based on the remaining principal ($12,827.64), applying $173.65 to the principal and $96.21 as interest. After five years, you'll have paid $3,191.60 in interest for borrowing $13,000. The example that follows covers only the first year of monthly payments on the $13,000 loan.

AMORTIZATION TABLE

PAYMENT NO.	PAYMENT	PRINCIPAL	INTEREST	BALANCE
1	269.86	172.36	97.50	12,827.64
2	269.86	173.65	96.21	12,653.99
3	269.86	174.96	94.91	12,479.00
4	269.86	176.27	93.59	12,302.77
5	269.86	177.59	92.27	12,125.18
6	269.86	178.92	90.94	11,946.26
7	269.86	180.26	89.60	11,765.99
8	269.86	181.62	88.25	11,584.38
9	269.86	182.98	86.88	11,401.40
10	269.86	184.35	85.51	11,217.05
11	269.86	185.73	84.13	11,031.32
12	269.86	187.13	82.74	10,844.19

The advantage of a fixed-rate loan is that regardless of how high other interest rates soar, your loan isn't affected. The disadvantage is that if other interest rates plummet during your repayment period, yours won't. Discuss your options with a number of lender banks.

Other Fees

Besides interest, you may also have to pay an application fee, a credit-check fee, and other miscellaneous fees for your loan. Ask about fees *before* applying for the loan. Some loans carry no fees. You could save a few hundred dollars by shopping around.

Collateral or Security

Few loans are made on the mere promise by the borrower that the money will be repaid with interest. Most loans are *secured,* which means you give the bank an ownership right in your property should you fail to make the loan payments *(default).* This is called your *collateral.*

Most borrowers put up collateral that is related to the loan. Sometimes that is the only way to get the loan or "financing." Thus, if you take out an auto loan, the car may be your collateral. If you fail to make the payments, the bank can repossess your car to sell it and repay the loan, the interest, and any fees you still owe. You may also use as collateral property you already own, such as a house, stocks, bonds, or your savings account.

If a bank makes you an *unsecured* loan, it can sue if you default. However, the bank must go through a legal process to get a court's judgment against you. It cannot simply "cash in" your collateral. Your chances of getting an unsecured loan are greater if:

• The loan principal is small
• The term of the loan is short
• You're willing to pay higher-than-average interest
• You are personally known to the bank officer

If you apply for an unsecured loan, you'll have to fill out a statement of financial worth. Also, the bank will not give you such a loan unless you are cleared by a national credit-reporting bureau, a company that keeps records of people's credit histories (see page 42).

To get other types of loans—for college tuition, home improvement, dental care, a vacation—many people use their home for collateral. When they make consumer loans, banks are reluctant to take anything but real property as collateral. In making commercial loans, however, they some-times accept business assets as collateral.

Default
Your loan contract will have a default clause that explains rights or remedies if you miss payments or violate other

provisions. Standard reasons banks resort to the default clause include:

- Lying on the loan application
- Declaring bankruptcy
- Failure to make a specified number of payments

Many default clauses include an *acceleration* provision that lets the bank sue you for the balance of the amount you owe if you are found in default. The logic is that you broke the agreement and, as a result, the bank wants out. It can ask a court to require you to pay in one lump sum all the money you owe. If you can't, the bank can sell the property you named as collateral and keep the money as repayment of the entire loan. When you negotiate a loan, therefore, it's important to understand how you can avoid default. If you ever find yourself in danger of defaulting, immediately inquire about your legal rights, including your right to a *grace period* in your contract and all the rights you have under the Fair Debt Collection Practices Act, discussed on page 41.

Prepayment
Some loan contracts include a prepayment penalty that allows the bank to charge you the full interest you would have owed for the entire life of the loan even if you pay it off early. If your contract includes such a prepayment penalty, you won't save interest and finance charges by prepaying the loan. It is to your advantage *not to* have this penalty clause.

Cosigning a Loan
Cosigners guarantee that they will pay off a loan if the principal borrower fails to pay. Cosigners are legally responsible for the full value of the loan, plus all late fees and penalties. In many states, lenders can even collect from co-

signers whether or not they've tried to collect from the principal borrowers.

Warning: Consider your full liability before you cosign any loan. The Federal Trade Commission found in 1986 that in three out of every four cosigned loans that defaulted, cosigners were asked to repay them. If you're considering cosigning a loan for someone else, have as much of the following language incorporated into your loan agreement as you can:

- Ask the lender to notify you if a payment is missed by the principal borrower.
- Get copies of all important documents, including the truth-in-lending disclosure statement (see page 39), the contract, and all attachments.
- Ask that your responsibility for the loan be limited to the principal only, thereby avoiding having to pay late charges, interest, and penalties.

SHOPPING FOR A LOAN

When you shop for a loan, talk with loan officers at several banks. Be sure to tell them how much you need and your ideal repayment schedule so they can fashion the loan to meet your needs as closely as possible. For instance, one person may want low payments and a loan that is stretched out over 10 years. Someone else may want to pay off the loan in as few years as possible. Be specific about your needs.

The bank officer will estimate the terms of the loan and call you to complete the application. Only after you actually apply for the loan will the bank tell you the interest rate, how long you have to repay it, and the requirements for collateral. This is called *pricing* the loan.

CONSUMER PROTECTIONS

Many consumer protection laws apply to loans. These include federal laws that prohibit discrimination and regulate debt collection practices, the Truth in Lending Act, and Federal Reserve Board regulations. States have enacted laws as well.

Truth in Lending

This law is contained within the *Consumer Credit Protection Act.* Under its provisions, whenever you apply for credit, whether it is a loan for home improvements, a mortgage, or a credit card, the lender is required to inform you in writing about certain terms and conditions *before you sign.* This allows you to evaluate different lenders' terms and assures that you know exactly how much you'll have to pay.

The law is extremely detailed. It specifies each term that must be disclosed and exactly how it must appear on the disclosure form. One of the two most important terms that must be disclosed to you under the law is the *finance charge,* the amount you pay to take out the loan. This includes the interest, service charges, and any appraisal charges (in the case of mortgages). The law also requires that this finance charge appear more conspicuously (in either boldfaced or larger type) than other items on the form.

The second important term is the *annual percentage rate* (APR). This translates the monthly interest you'll pay into the effective rate you'll be charged for an entire year. It, too, must be displayed more prominently than the other terms on the form.

For example: You borrow $1,000 for a year and pay a finance charge of $80. If you were to pay the whole loan off at once at the end of the year, your APR would be 8%, but loans rarely work this way. People usually pay loans back in equal monthly installments. In this case that would be $90 each month. This means you don't really get to "use" all of the $1,000 for the entire year but a declining amount of it each month, thereby in effect paying a higher interest rate— the APR. In this example, the APR would be 14.5%.

The Truth in Lending Act requires that consumers be given this information so they can more easily calculate and compare terms.

Another provision in the Consumer Credit Protection Act allows you to cancel your loan contract within three business days of signing it if you used your home as collateral. This "right of rescission," or "cooling-off" period, is to allow you to reconsider whether you want to risk your home as collateral. Any or no reason is enough for canceling the loan agreement. However, your cancellation has to be in writing. You may waive this right, but again, you must do so in writing.

Equal Credit Opportunity Act

Under this federal law, it is illegal to discriminate against loan applicants because of their sex, marital status, race, color, age, religion, national origin, or receipt of public assistance. For example, the law forbids loan officers to ask about a woman's childbearing intentions or to ignore alimony and child-support income in calculating her ability to repay a loan. The law also protects borrowers from retaliation when they exercise their rights under federal credit laws.

Under the Act, lenders *can* ask questions about your ability to repay, such as your wages, place of employment, occupation, how long you have been employed, your monthly expenses, your credit history, outstanding debts, and whether you pay your bills on time. They can also ask for a list of your assets. A lender who goes beyond this violates the law and can be taken to court by the state attorney general; or you can sue that lender for damages, a penalty, and your lawyer's fees.

Fair Debt Collection Practices Act

The law spells out the limits on what a "debt collector" can do in pressuring you to pay a debt. Prohibited tactics include threats of violence, repeated use of the telephone to harass you, publication of a debt, making false statements about your credit history, and discussing your debt with your neighbors or coworkers. Lawyers who engage in debt collection were exempt from this law until it was amended in 1986. Now, they, too, are covered. Violations should be reported to the Federal Trade Commission (Appendix III).

Credit Practices Rule

This rule applies to finance companies, department stores, car dealers, and others. It does not specifically apply to banks. Similar rules created by the Federal Reserve Board do, however, cover some banks. Administered by the Federal Trade Commission, they forbid lenders from adding certain anticonsumer provisions to credit agreements. For example, you cannot be asked to sign away your right to be notified of a court hearing in the event your creditor sues you for nonpayment (called a confession-of-judgment clause). Nor can you waive your right to keep personal belongings exempt from creditors under the bankruptcy laws. The law also identifies information that must be disclosed to cosigners of a loan and limits on the late fees that can be charged.

Fair Credit Reporting Act

If you have ever applied for credit, you have been protected by this law. Under its provisions, all institutions to which you apply for credit—banks, loan companies, department stores—prepare a "credit history" and send it to "credit bureaus." Credit bureaus keep computer files of these credit histories. Under this law, you have a right to a free copy of any credit report that has been used by any creditor as the basis for denying you credit. The law also requires that, with certain exceptions, unfavorable information must be eliminated from your record after seven years. You also have the right to correct any mistakes in the bureau's credit history of you. If the bureau still insists you have a credit "blemish," you can include in your file a letter of explanation that must be sent along with future credit inquiries to lenders.

State Protections

Each state has its own official who regulates banks, typically called the Commissioner or Superintendent of Banking and Financial Institutions. State laws overlap federal laws, but if a conflict arises, usually federal law prevails.

State laws sometimes give more protection to borrowers than their federal counterparts. For example, some states' banking laws require lenders to exhaust all avenues of collection from the principal borrower before trying to collect from a cosigner. In some states, you cannot waive your right to exempt from collection certain pieces of property, such as your home and car. And in all states, you cannot waive your right to be notified of a court hearing if you're sued for nonpayment. Whenever state law gives you protections *in addition to* the federal laws, those protections will be upheld as well.

State banking authorities regulate interest rates and charges and penalties such as late fees. State Consumer Protection Agencies and attorneys general monitor discrimination in credit and often investigate illegal credit practices by finance and credit card companies and, occasionally, banks. They sue offenders as necessary.

These authorities and agencies can be helpful, especially with the laws unique to your state (see Appendix III). In particular, some state agencies offer pamphlets in several languages on banking laws. In California, for example, the superintendent of banks provides pamphlets in English, Chinese, and Spanish. Other states provide pamphlets in languages common in their areas.

CHAPTER 6

SOLVING PROBLEMS

Although many state and federal laws govern lending and credit, there are few places that will help in resolving a lending dispute. This section explains where you can go and discusses the two major federal agencies that investigate banks. Although these agencies do not handle individual complaints, they do investigate and penalize banks that break the law.

COMMON PROBLEMS

People have three common legal problems with lenders: being turned down for a loan for an illegal reason, finding out they owe much more than they anticipated because of inadequate loan disclosures, and illegal collection techniques.

Loan Rejection

If you have been turned down for a loan, ask your loan officer why. A responsible loan officer will show you the financial criteria used to make the decision and even discuss with you the loan committee's denial. If the decision was based on incorrect information about your credit record, ask to have the loan reconsidered. Submit a letter explaining the error. Also, be sure to correct the information if a credit bureau was involved.

If you suspect that the bank turned down the loan for an illegal reason, such as your race or sex, talk to the loan officer's supervisor. Any questions or discussion about your ethnic origin, marital status, religion, or the like should be reported to the supervisor. If your application is still denied, file a claim of discrimination with the local, state, or federal agency that handles discrimination in credit. You should also notify the bank's regulatory authority.

If you've been turned down for a loan, the Equal Credit Opportunity Act requires the lender to give you the name of the regulatory agency that you can complain to.

Every state, many counties, and most major cities have an office that handles individuals' credit-discrimination complaints. Each one operates under a different law, and the laws overlap, but usually state and local laws forbid more "bases" of discrimination. For example, while a state or local law may prohibit discrimination based on political affiliation, federal law does not, so if you've been turned down because of your political-party registration, check with local or state authorities; federal law won't help you.

Also, each agency has a different deadline by which you must file a complaint after being turned down. Call your local Office of Consumer Affairs to find out about deadlines, where to file your complaint, and the rules and procedures that apply. If you're unsure where to file, contact the Consumer Affairs Office of the Federal Reserve Bank nearest you and ask for a referral (see Appendix III).

Agencies that investigate claims of discrimination will negotiate with the bank and may hold a conference to determine if you have been rejected illegally. Both you and the bank officials will have to attend this conference, and although most people do not hire a lawyer to represent them, if lots of money is at stake, you might want to consider that course. If you win, depending on your state, you can collect damages plus a penalty and your attorney's fees.

The law also requires you to exhaust your administrative remedies before litigating. That means you must take your claim to one of these agencies before you can sue in court.

Women and Credit Problems

Women have been frequent victims of credit discrimination. Lenders have refused to loan money to single women, women of childbearing age, and women who received alimony or child-support income. The Equal Credit Opportunity Act forbids such activities. If you find yourself the victim of discrimination because of your sex, follow the suggestions above and contact a local or national women's organization to ask where you can go for help locally.

Inadequate Disclosures

If the bank failed to give you the disclosures required by the federal Truth in Lending Act, you have two recourses: Get the bank to agree to the terms as you understood them or get out of the loan. Your local Consumer Affairs Office or the Consumer Affairs Division of your State Attorney General's Office may investigate such claims. If so, either one may have authority to negotiate an agreement with the bank on your behalf. If not, or if negotiation doesn't resolve the problem, your only recourse is to sue.

If the paperwork is in order, these cases are fairly simple. But, as in all court cases, they take time and can be expensive. If you win, you'll be able to collect damages plus a penalty.

Collection Problems

If your bank is using illegal collection methods, such as trying to accelerate the loan after only one missed payment, and it is unwilling to listen to reason, again you should complain to your local Consumer Affairs Office or the State Attorney General's Office. They will both be familiar with collection laws. Most such agencies also handle individual collection complaints. Again, if this doesn't solve the problem, you'll have to go to court.

REGULATORY AGENCIES

Several federal and state agencies regulate banking and credit. Most of them can give you information about the law, some will refer you to agencies where you can file a formal complaint, and all of them keep records on violations of the banking and lending laws they enforce. If a bank shows a pattern of violating the law, these agencies can bring suit to stop the illegal behavior, impose fines, and, if the bank's illegal behavior persists, close it down.

If you complain to one of these agencies, it will contact the bank about the practice. This may be enough to get your complaint resolved informally.

The two major federal agencies that regulate lending and credit are the Federal Reserve Board and the Federal Trade Commission. If these don't handle your problem, they will refer you to the federal or state agency that does.

The Federal Reserve Board oversees its member banks' compliance with federal laws like Truth in Lending and the Credit Practices Rule. Most banks are members of the Federal Reserve System. If you complain to "the Fed" and learn that your bank is not a member, your complaint will be referred to the appropriate agency within 15 days. The Federal Reserve has free information on the laws that govern lending and credit (see Appendix III for regional offices).

The Federal Trade Commission (FTC) monitors compliance with federal laws by nonbank lenders, like credit unions and retail store credit departments. The FTC also has free literature about your rights under credit protection laws.

Finally, every bank is responsible to a federal government agency that monitors its activity. Although none of these agencies can resolve individual disputes, all of them can and will apply pressure when appropriate. A little pressure from one of them can make all the difference in the world. If you were turned down for a loan, you should have received one of these addresses from the lender. If you didn't, the lender is violating the Equal Credit Opportunity Act; ask your local Office of Consumer Protection or the Federal Reserve Bank regional office nearest you what agency you should complain to. These include:

Comptroller of the Currency
Consumer Affairs Division
490 L'Enfant Plaza, E SW
Washington, DC 20219
(202) 447-1810
(For national banks)

Federal Deposit Insurance
  Corporation (FDIC)
Consumer Affairs Division
550 17th St. NW
Washington, DC 20429
(800) 424-5488
(For non–Federal Reserve state
  banks)

Office of Thrift Supervision
  (OTS)
Consumer Affairs Division
1700 G St. NW
Washington, DC 20552
(202) 906-6237
(For federally insured savings
  and loans)

National Credit Union
  Administration
Consumer Affairs Division
1776 G St NW, Suite 800
Washington, DC 20006
(202) 682-1900
(For Federal credit unions)

RESOURCES

Many of these materials are offered free, some for a nominal fee. For best service, call or write for an order form and mail it in with your request.

From the Federal Trade Commission
Bureau of Consumer Protection, Washington, DC 20580. (202) 326-3650.

Buying and Borrowing: Cash in on the Facts
Credit Billing Errors? Use FCBA (Fair Credit Billing Act)
Credit Practices Rule, Facts for Consumers
Equal Credit Opportunity, Facts for Consumers
Fair Debt Collection, Facts for Consumers
Fair Credit Billing
Fair Credit Reporting
Fix Your Own Credit Problems and Save Money
Solving Credit Problems

From the Federal Reserve Board
Board of Governors, Federal Reserve, 20th and Constitution Ave. NW, Washington, DC 20551. (202) 452-3000.

A Guide to Federal Reserve Regulations
Consumer Credit Terminology Handbook
Consumer Handbook to Credit Protection Laws
Federal Reserve Glossary
The Story of Banks and Thrifts
Truth in Lending Simplified
What Truth in Lending Means to You

Other Materials

Tips on Saving and Investing, Tips on Consumer Credit.
Council of Better Business Bureaus, Inc., Consumer Information Services, 1515 Wilson Blvd., Arlington, VA 22209.
(703) 276-0100.

The Bank Book. Naphtali Hoffman and Stephen Brobeck.
Consumer Federation of America, Harcourt Brace Jovano-
vich, 757 Third Ave., New York, NY 10017. (212) 614-3000.
1986. 222 pages.

CHAPTER 7

CONTRACT LANGUAGE

The contract explained in this chapter is for a standard, multipurpose loan from a bank. Other kinds of loans, such as those from finance companies that work through car dealers, large-appliance distributors, and mortgage companies, will have similar if not identical terms.

You cannot write your own loan contract with banks because, unfortunately, they will not accept it. You'll probably be stuck with a standard, single-page form that comes with five or six different-colored carbon copies. It will have a great deal of fine print, all of which is explained in this chapter. When presented with such a standard form, the best you will probably be able to negotiate is elimination of some provisions.

Because most loan forms are multipurpose, when complete, your form probably will have some blank spaces, where portions don't apply to your loan. Be sure to mark them clearly: "N/A," for "not applicable."

THE "MAGIC BOX"

The front of the loan form lists the financial terms of the contract: the costs of the loan, including principal, interest, fees, insurance costs, interest rate, late charges, prepayment options or penalties, security interest, and space for the signatures. These terms are usually contained in what is called the "Magic Box," set off from the rest of the contract. The Magic Box is intended to make sure these terms are "clear and conspicuous" and separated from the other items on the form, as required by the Truth in Lending Act.

This example includes only those items required by the law. Some lenders choose to add other information as well. The following list describes all of the items you are likely to find in the "Magic Box" on the loan contract you are offered—both those required and those not required.

Borrower(s)—This is you, your spouse, and anyone else who is a borrower, and your address.

Lender—The law requires that the lender's name be disclosed on the form. Most lenders also include their address. Under the law, lenders are permitted to call themselves either "creditor" or "lender."

Annual Percentage Rate
The cost of my credit as a yearly rate.
_____ %

Annual Percentage Rate (APR)—Your contract will include the words "Annual Percentage Rate." Required by law, this is the interest rate for the declining balance for each year of the loan. Remember, if you have a fluctuating interest rate, the APR will not remain the same throughout the life of the loan. In that case, the contract will state that the rate is "fluctuating." If it's a fixed rate, the percentage will be fixed for the period stated in the contract, typically one, two, or three years.

When calculating the APR of a fixed-rate loan, it's important to note that it is an *annual* interest rate, not a lifetime rate. This means that if the loan is taken out at 10%, one twelfth of 10% interest of the unpaid principal is charged

Annual Percentage Rate	Finance Charge	Amount Financed	Total of Payments
The cost of my credit as a yearly rate. ___%	The dollar amount the credit will cost me. $ ___	The amount of credit provided to me or on my behalf. $ ___	The amount I will have paid after I have made all the payments as scheduled. $ ___

My payment schedule will be:

Number of Payments	Amount of Payments	When Payments Are Due
	$	Monthly beginning ___
	$	

Security: (Applicable box(es) checked)

☐ I am giving you a security interest in my real estate located at:

Street_____ City_____ State_____ Zip_____

☐ I am giving you a security interest in my motor vehicle identified as follows:

Year_____ Make_____ Model_____ Body Type_____ Serial No._____

Demand: If this box is checked ☐, this obligation is payable on demand.

I acknowledge that the bank has a right of setoff against my accounts, except IRAs and Keogh accounts.

Filing Fees: $ _____   **Late Charge:** If a payment is more than fifteen (15) days late, I will be responsible for a late charge of 5% of the payment.

Prepayment: If I pay off early, I will not have to pay a penalty, and if I have already paid any prepaid finance charge, I will not be entitled to receive a refund of any or all of the prepaid finance charge.

I will purchase: ☐Credit Life Insurance ☐Credit Disability Insurance

I can see the contract documents for additional information about nonpayment, default, any required payment before the scheduled date, and prepayment refunds and penalties.

each month, turning your effective annual rate into considerably more than 10%.

Finance Charge
The dollar amount the credit will cost me.
$ _____

Finance Charge—This section must show in dollars and cents the amount you will pay for the loan, including any costs, such as insurance "hidden" in your monthly payments. The law also requires a brief definition of terms. Most banks will use the phrase "The dollar amount the credit will cost me." This must be more conspicuously displayed than the other information, and lenders must use the exact words "Finance Charge." They usually put them in bold face and inside a border.

Amount Financed
The amount of credit provided to me or on my behalf.
$ _____

Amount Financed—This term must be used to describe the total amount of the loan and any other money the bank is lending you to pay for costs.

Total of Payments
The amount I will have paid after I have made all the payments as scheduled.
$ _____

Total of Payments—This is the total amount of money you will have paid after the loan is paid off. It includes finance charges, the principal, insurance, and all other costs. For a three-year, 10% interest loan of $12,000, the total of all payments is $13,939.56.

Number of Payments

Amount of Payments
$
$

When Payments Are Due
Monthly beginning

Payment Schedule—Here you will find: the total number of payments, the amount of those payments, and when they are due. Most banks do not list each payment separately unless the payment amounts vary.

Security: (*Applicable box(es) checked*)

I am giving you a security interest in my real estate located at:
Street:_____
City:_____County:_____
State:_____Zip:_____

   I am giving you a security interest in my motor vehicle identified as follows:

Year:_____Make:_____
Model:_____Body Type:_____
Serial Number:_____

   Other (describe)_____
_____

Security—The typical Magic Box also identifies any security or collateral you are putting up. If the loan is a secured loan, the property that is to serve as the collateral must be disclosed. If the loan is secured by the item being financed, the collateral will be described as "the property purchased in this transaction." If it is other property, it must be described in specific detail. Many creditors will be precise here to protect themselves. If a loan is unsecured, put "N/A" in these blanks.

> This obligation is payable on DEMAND ☐

Demand Feature—Check your agreement to see if it says your loan will be "payable on demand." If it does, the bank can legally require you to pay the full amount of the principal and interest you owe *any time it chooses.* If that's the case, the law requires the bank to inform you on the front of the loan. A bank officer usually checks a box for this purpose. If your loan is not payable on demand, be sure to write "N/A" in that box.

Most consumer loans are installment loans that do not include "payment on demand." However, a demand clause on the back of the agreement often gives the lender the right to "call in" the loan if you default on one or more payments. This is different from the payment-on-demand feature in the Magic Box, which must be disclosed.

> I acknowledge that the bank has a right of setoff against my accounts, except IRAs and Keogh accounts.

This sentence applies when the bank has a security interest that gives it the right to collect from accounts you have at the bank. Federal law forbids collecting from Individual Retirement Accounts (IRAs) and Keogh accounts (self-employment retirement accounts). These terms are spelled out in more detail on the back of the loan agreement.

> Filing Fees: ___*(amount of fee)*___

Filing Fees—Loan application fees and other such charges are listed here. Most other costs, such as interest, are already factored into the "Amount Financed" and are not included here. Frequently, application fees are nominal.

> Late Charge: If a payment is more than fifteen (15) days late, I will be responsible for a late charge of 5% of the payment.

Late Charge—Late fees must be explained here. Many states' banking laws prescribe the maximum late charges that can be collected, usually a percentage ceiling, such as 5%. Grace periods are common and almost all forms list them here, but the law doesn't require it.

> Prepayment: If I pay off early, I will not have to pay a penalty, and if I have already paid any prepaid finance charge, I will not be entitled to receive a refund of any or all of the prepaid finance charge.

Prepayment—If a fee is charged when you make loan payments early, it must be stated here. If no penalty is charged, that, too, must be stated. Most consumer loans allow prepayment, but none of them will refund that part of the finance charge that you've already paid. Thus, if you pay off your loan early, you'll end up paying a somewhat higher interest rate even if you aren't charged a penalty, because your early payments included interest on the full term of the loan.

> I will purchase: ☐ Credit Life Insurance
> ☐ Credit Disability Insurance

Insurance—You may want, or be required by the lender, to buy insurance that will pay off the balance of your loan if you die or become disabled. Insurance isn't required by law, but your lender may require it, especially from borrowers who make small down payments on home mortgages. If you are buying insurance as a hedge against default, either because the bank requires it or because you want it, the law does require that it and its cost be listed on the loan form.

If it isn't required by the lender, the decision of whether or not to buy insurance should be based on your assessment of the risk. If yours is a two-income household and either of you earns enough to pay all monthly bills including the loan, you probably don't need insurance. If the death or disability of one spouse would spell financial ruin, however, you may want to consider it.

> I can see the contract documents for additional information about nonpayment, default, any required payment before the scheduled date, and prepayment refunds and penalties.

This is called the contract reference section. The lender must cite the other documents or other parts of the contract wherever relevant. For instance, if you are giving collateral, the security agreement must be mentioned next to the identification of the collateral on the loan form.

Itemization of Amount Financed—Lenders are required by law to give notice on the loan form that borrowers can request a written itemization of payments. Most lenders, however, go beyond this minimum disclosure requirement and print the itemization directly on the agreement. Many of the blanks on the itemization section are for specific kinds of loans, such as mortgages, car loans, or home-improve-

ITEMIZED LIST

Itemization of Amount Financed:

Amount paid directly to me	$ _____
Amount paid to others for me	_____
Credit life insurance	_____
Credit accident and health insurance	_____
Credit report fee	_____
Title examination fee	_____
Appraisal fee	_____
Title insurance	_____
Recording fees	_____
Notary fee	_____
Automobile license, title and registration	_____
Other	_____
Subtotal	$ _____
Less prepaid amounts (paid by me—	
application fee, finance charge)	$ _____
TOTAL	$ _____

ment loans. Make sure the appropriate blanks are completed on your form and the others marked "N/A."

BACK OF THE FORM

The back of your loan form is probably wall-to-wall "fine print." This is where the lender describes fully the specific terms of the loan. As noted earlier, many if not all of the terms on the front of the form are legally required. Few federal and state laws apply to the loan terms on the back, however. As you read them, notice that now, many lenders at least try to use plain language, compared to what was true only a few years ago.

> Definitions or Meanings of Words—The words "I," "me," "we," and "my" mean all borrowers to this agreement and all guarantors. "You" and "your" mean the bank and its successors and assigns.

All contracts have a definitions section. The term *borrower* is used to mean all signers except the witnesses and the bank. When a loan is guaranteed by someone other than the borrower, that *guarantor* is considered to be your legal backer. If you don't pay, your guarantor owes the money.

Real estate mortgages are often *sold.* When a bank sells your loan, the new owner (called the *successor* or *assign*) steps into the shoes of the original lender and takes on the same rights and obligations as that original lender.

> Applicable Law—This note shall be governed by the laws of the state in which it is signed. Terms which do not comply with the laws of that state shall not be effective. If a term shall be deemed invalid, it shall not affect the validity of the remainder of this agreement.

This adds nothing to the contract. It merely tells you that the contract must obey state laws. It notifies you that if the bank has agreed to a term that's illegal in your state, that term is void, but not the rest of the contract.

> Payments—I agree to pay all the principal and interest of this loan as set forth in the payment schedule. I agree that each scheduled payment I make shall be applied against the unpaid balance as described in the amortization schedule provided. In addition, I agree that payments made by me shall be applied first to late payments or penalties, if any, then to interest and then to principal.

This obligates you to make payments according to the payment schedule in the loan. Most loans include a payment schedule in the agreement. This language also tells you how much of each scheduled payment is applied to the interest. For large loans, early payments are applied almost entirely to paying off the interest, with only a small portion to the principal.

The bank will probably supply you a schedule of payments. If it doesn't, ask for one. This itemizes the interest and principal you will pay at each step along the way. It can be especially useful in calculating income-tax deductions for the mortgage interest you pay.

> Default—I will be in default if: (1) I fail to make any payment when it is due under this agreement, (2) any representation or statement made by me under this agreement is false, (3) I file for bankruptcy or insolvency, or receivership proceedings are begun against me or any other collection attempts are made against any of my property, whether through legal process or not, (4) I die or am declared incompetent, (5) I violate any security agreement by selling or transferring any of the property of which you have been given a security interest without your permission, (6) I fail to keep any other promise in the agreement, (7) a judgment of any kind is obtained against me.

This is standard default language, and all of the listed reasons for default are typical. They define when the bank can find that you have broken the loan agreement and what the bank can do about it. Most banks will not negotiate any changes in this section.

Be sure you know exactly what you are agreeing to. Pay particular attention to how default is defined and what the bank may do if you are found in default. However, the bank has the option of triggering the default clause; whether it does so or not is up to the bank.

Typically, failing to make one payment is not enough to cause a bank to find you in default. More likely, you'll be charged a late fee. Most banks prefer that you pay back the loan as agreed, so they will wait through the grace period, or even longer, before moving for default. However, if you lie or omit to tell part of the truth on your loan application, especially about your credit history, the bank may well start default proceedings if you miss one or more payments. If you file for bankruptcy or are successfully sued by another creditor for default, this, too, will cause a bank to consider your loan in default.

In this agreement, as is standard, you are in default if you die. All payments become the property of your estate and beneficiaries, and your heirs may want to negotiate with the bank to continue to pay in installments. Some loans are forgiven or canceled at death, but most are not, unless you purchased life insurance that pays off your loan in full.

This section also allows default if a court declares you mentally incompetent, but you should be aware that this has been successfully challenged in some states, based on laws that prohibit discrimination against the mentally disabled.

If you sign a security agreement, it's standard for the bank to require that you agree not to sell or give away whatever property you've put up as collateral for the loan. If you do sell or give it away, the bank has the right to move for default.

Most banks also include a catchall statement that you can be found in default if you don't live up to the terms of the loan contract.

Finally, if a judgment is entered against you—that is, if another creditor to whom you owe money sues you and wins—the bank will be able to have you declared in default.

In the event of my default, you may do any of the following:

Acceleration—You may accelerate the loan, declaring all unpaid sums under the loan immediately due,

Collection—You may take any legal action to collect the loan and charge me for all court costs and reasonable attorneys' fees,

Set-off—You may offset any amounts that I owe against any account that I maintain with you, with the exception of tax-deferred retirement accounts. In addition, you shall not be liable for dishonor of a check for insufficient funds in the event you exercise this right, or

Exercise any other rights you have under the law.

If you are in default of the loan, the bank can use the *acceleration clause* to make the entire loan due immediately. However, if you make one or two late payments, that's usually not enough to cause the bank to accelerate your loan. If it tries, contact the loan officer to correct the mistake.

If the lender sues you to collect the loan, this language requires that, if you lose, you'll have to pay the lender's attorneys' fees. That's standard, but if you can get a loan without this language, do so; you will save yourself money even if you default.

If the lender wins a court judgment finding you in default, it can sell any of your secured property, seize any bank accounts you have in its banks (except tax-sheltered retirement accounts), garnish and attach your wages, even try to seize other property of yours to pay off the debt. If the bank seizes money in your account, you are responsible for any costs that result, such as bounced-check charges. But banks can't pressure you to deposit your savings in their banks simply so they can exercise this right. If one does pressure you, report it to a Consumer Affairs Office.

Prepayment—I may prepay all or part of this loan at any time. Prepayment will not change any of the dates due or amount of payments. There will be no prepayment penalty and no refund of prepaid finance charges.

This prepayment language is standard. If you pay double on one monthly payment, you still must make the full payment next month, but you'll be lowering the total interest you'll eventually pay.

As noted earlier, prepayment clauses define your responsibility if you wish to pay off the loan early. In this contract, you aren't required to pay additional interest or other charges if you prepay. Many loans, like this one, do allow you to prepay with no penalties, but even so you won't get any refund of any charges already paid (excepting payment for insurance, as noted below). Also, your effective annual interest will be higher because your early payments were for interest across the entire life of the loan.

> Late Payments—I agree to pay a late charge of 5% if any payment is received by you more than fifteen (15) days after the payment due date.

This gives you a 15-day "grace" period for late payments, with no late fee. State law commonly requires such a penalty-free period. Be sure your loan includes such a grace period and let the bank officer know what time of the month is most convenient for you to make your payments.

> Insurance—I agree to purchase credit life insurance, if required by you for this loan as described in the itemization of the amount financed. This purchase shall be made through a company licensed to do business in this state and approved by you. Such insurance will cover only those person(s) signing this note. Insurance coverage shall begin when this note is signed and shall expire on the original maturity date of this note, unless there is a prepayment. In the event of prepayment, I shall be entitled to a refund of a portion of the insurance premium.

Some lenders require you to take out "credit life insurance" that pays off the loan if you die or, in some cases, are severely disabled. Some loans, like student loans, are canceled if the borrower dies. Most, however, become the debt of the person's heirs unless paid off by insurance. If you're required to get insurance, expect to be urged to buy it from a company of the lender's choosing, but you are free to buy it from any licensed insurer or agent. In fact, you probably can save a little money by shopping around. Insurance can add anywhere from $5 to $50 a month to your payments, depending on the size of the loan insured.

Credit life-insurance premiums are computed as part of the loan repayment. Federal law requires that the Magic Box on the front of the loan form include a disclosure of the cost of the insurance. Lenders usually require insurance for an unsecured loan and for mortgage loans when the down payment is small.

You may be able to convince your lender not to require credit life insurance. Ask your loan officer what criteria are used to determine who must buy it. Remember: It is illegal to make this decision based on your race, age, sex, national origin, marital status, or source of income. It is legal, however, to make it based on your credit record, your income, or other objective evidence of your ability to pay. If you feel you are being discriminated against, talk to a state or local Office of Consumer Affairs or Human Rights.

> Borrowers' Waivers—I waive presentment, demand, notice of dishonor, and protest except where prohibited by applicable law.

Every loan contains this condition. Waiving "presentment and demand" means relinquishing your right to be billed separately for each payment. Instead, lenders often provide a coupon book with tear-out coupons for each payment. When your loan is due at the bank's discretion (*demand* loans), this clause isn't included.

Waiving notice of "dishonor and protest" means giving up your right to be notified that you are late with your payments or have otherwise violated the agreement and that the lender intends to collect the full balance due.

> My signature on the reverse side of this note acknowledges that I have read this note and all the disclosures required by law and that I agree to all its conditions.

This is a statement by you that you have read and agree to all the terms of the loan. If you have signed the loan agreement, or *note,* there is a legal presumption that you know and understand all its terms. This language is simply the bank's way of reinforcing this presumption and putting you on notice of its effect.

> Confession of Judgment—I authorize an attorney that you designate to appear on behalf of me in court in the event I default, and obtain a judgment for the unpaid balance of this loan. I waive any right I may have to notice and authorize you, upon obtaining such judgment, to immediately execute such judgment.

This statement is *illegal* under the federal Credit Practices Rule for consumer loans. If it appears in your agreement, it is void. Once popular with lenders, such a provision waives your right to defend against a lawsuit if you violate the default clause. It allows the lender to have any attorney it chooses go to court in your place and accept a judgment against you. This in turn allows the lender to take your property without even informing you that you're being sued. *Any lender who needs to be reminded that this provision is illegal should be avoided at all costs.*

SECURITY AGREEMENT

I grant you a security interest in the collateral described on the front of this agreement to secure the loan obligation arising from the loan.

This explains that if you fail to pay or otherwise violate the agreement, you are allowing the bank to sell the property you've put up as collateral and listed as such in this agreement.

Protection of the Property/Purpose—I agree to keep the collateral in good order and repair and will not use it in violation of the law. I shall not permit others to use the collateral in violation of the law or this agreement. I understand that the collateral is to be used for consumer purposes only and any other use shall be a violation of this agreement.

This protects the bank's interest in your collateral. It requires that you keep the collateral—be it a home or a car or a pleasure boat—in good repair and not use it for business purposes, unless, of course, that use is permitted in the contract. Obviously, the collateral will be no good to the bank if it is damaged or lost.

Use and Maintenance—I will not sell, lease or otherwise dispose of the collateral without your written prior approval. I agree to keep the property in the jurisdiction where I reside, except if the collateral is an automobile, I may use it outside the jurisdiction for temporary periods of normal usage.

I agree that I shall abide by the terms of any insurance to which the collateral is subject.

This is more typical language to protect the bank's interest in the collateral. It requires you to get the bank's written approval before you do anything that changes your control over the collateral, by selling it, for example. This doesn't mean you can never sell or lease your collateral. You can, as long as the bank agrees or you pay off the loan immediately and thus settle your debt. Any substitution of collateral will have to be approved by the lender in writing and in advance.

This also obliges you to keep the collateral in the state where you live, except in the case of automobiles, which are allowed to be used outside the state for normal purposes.

> Payment of Taxes and Fees—I agree to pay all taxes, fees or other charges which come due on the property. If I fail to pay taxes and fees due on the collateral, you have the right under this agreement to make these payments for me and I will become immediately obligated to reimburse you for these costs. These amounts shall become an additional debt secured by the collateral and as such will immediately begin to accrue interest.

This allows the bank to protect its interest in the collateral by paying any fees or taxes that are due on it and to bill you, with interest, for reimbursement. If you are using your car as collateral, the bank may pay your insurance or registration fees. If your collateral is a condominium unit, the bank may step in and pay any fees that, if they weren't paid, could cause the loss of the unit or cause a lien to be placed against it. Don't confuse the "fees" referred to here with those, like application fees, due on the loan itself.

The bank will add to your loan payments any fees it pays and charge you interest on this additional "loan." Make sure that if you are refusing to pay a bill intentionally, the lender is told in writing and doesn't pay it against your wishes. For example, if the government is overcharging you because of a mixup in your property taxes, notify your lender in writing that you are withholding your payment and why.

> Insurance—I agree to keep the collateral insured for the full value against damage or loss with an insurance company ap-

proved by you. I shall make a copy of this policy available to you. Such policy shall designate you as the loss payee. I shall pay all premiums when they are due. If I fail to purchase insurance or fail to make timely payments, you have the right to make them and add such costs to the loan secured by this agreement. These costs shall accrue interest from the first day.

If the collateral is damaged or lost, you may, at your option, use any insurance proceeds to repair or replace the collateral and I will be responsible to repay, if any, the remaining amount of the loan.

Yet more standard language to protect the lender's interest in your collateral property: It requires you to insure the collateral using a policy approved by the bank. The bank will usually suggest insurers it is used to dealing with, but remember that you are free to get your own. If the collateral is damaged or stolen, the bank can collect the insurance payment. Here, you are also agreeing that if you fail to pay the premiums, the bank can do so and add it to the cost of the loan.

The insurance payment replaces the damaged or stolen collateral, which may turn out to be less than the amount of the loan. If the insurance payment is not enough to reimburse the bank completely, you'll have to make up the difference.

Inspection—I agree to permit you to inspect the collateral at any reasonable time.

Banks rarely inspect collateral. However, if the bank has reason to believe the property is lost or damaged, it may do so under this provision, as long as it is during normal business hours and you are given advance notice. If you feel you are being subjected to an unfair inspection, report it to the nearest Consumer Affairs Office and appropriate banking authority.

Remedies—If I default, you may, in addition to remedies listed above, take any of the following actions:

Repossess and repair the collateral without notice to me and without legal proceedings.

Require me to deliver the collateral to a place of your choosing.

Sell the collateral after providing me with 15 days' notice. Notice, for the purposes of this agreement, shall be considered given when it is put in the U.S. Mail, postage prepaid, addressed to anyone signing this agreement.

I shall be responsible for the costs of repossession and resale of the collateral and such costs shall be added to this obligation and interest shall accrue thereon. I shall also be responsible for any deficiency that results from a sale of the collateral.

This is also standard. It sets out the lender's rights to your collateral if you are found in default and allows the bank to sell the collateral without suing you or getting a court judgment. If you are in default, the lender may take the collateral from you, give you 15 days' notice, and sell it if you don't pay the balance of the loan within that 15 days.

Each state has a "repossession" law that sets out what procedures a lender can use to sell the collateral. In the District of Columbia, for example, you must be given 10 days' notice before your collateral can be taken, and another 15 days in which to bring your payments up to date before it can be sold. You must also be given the right to buy back the collateral any time before the actual sale.

Each state's law describes how lenders can seize the collateral (for example, they can't "disturb the peace") and how many days' notice they must give you before they can sell it (typically 15). Your local or state Consumer Affairs Office will be familiar with your state's "repo" law.

If you owe more than the lender can get from selling the repossessed collateral, you may be sued for the "deficiency." Many suits are for such repossession or deficiency judgments.

NOTICE OF YOUR RIGHT TO CANCEL

I am entering into a transaction that will result in a mortgage or security interest on my home. I have a legal right under federal law to cancel this transaction, without cost, within three business days from whichever of the following events occurs last:

(1) The date of the transaction, which is _____, or
(2) The date I received my disclosures under the Truth in Lending law,
(3) The date I received this notice of the right to cancel.

If I cancel this transaction, the mortgage or security interest is also cancelled. Within 20 calendar days after you receive notice, you must take the steps necessary to reflect the fact that the mortgage or security interest on my home has been cancelled, and you must return to me any money or property I have given to you or to anyone else in connection with this transaction.

If I decide to cancel this transaction, I may do so by notifying you in writing, at *(mailing address of lender)*.

I may use any written statement that is signed and dated by me and states my intention to cancel, or I may use this notice by dating and signing below.

If I cancel by mail or telegram, I must send the notice no later than midnight of *(date)*. If I send or deliver written notice to cancel some other way, it must be delivered to the above address no later than that time.

I Wish to Cancel.

(Your Name)	
Consumer's Signature	Date

The Borrower should keep one copy of this notice because it contains important information about the Borrower's rights.

If your loan is secured by your residence, the Truth in Lending Act requires that you be given a three-day "cooling-off" period after you sign a loan and be told about it by your lender. This gives you 72 hours to cancel it for any reason. Canceling means you also end any right the lender has to your home.

Because of this law, lenders prefer to wait three days before turning the money over to you and completing the paperwork. If you can't wait, you can waive the "cooling-off" period, but you must do so in writing.

PART III

IMPROVING YOUR HOME

CHAPTER 8

HOME WORK

Tom wants to replace his bathroom fixtures. He obtains four bids: two high, one low, and one in between.

Each morning at 6:00, Joan hears banging, sawing, and drilling from the house next door. She warns her neighbor to do something about the noise or she'll complain to the police.

Kate wants to install a swimming pool. A neighbor offers to do the work for half what a professional contractor would charge if Kate will buy the materials and get the building permit. Kate agrees and seals the deal with a handshake.

Undertaking major home improvements like these allows you to do something creative and personal with your environment, increases the value of your property, and can be less expensive than moving.

If you don't know what you're doing, however, or if you get stuck with an incompetent contractor, your home "improvement" can quickly turn into a home nightmare, spiraling you into debt, wreaking havoc in your life, and making you wish you'd spent the money on a trip to Bali instead. That's why it's important to make the effort to find a contractor who's well qualified, financially stable, and willing to sign a contract that spells out the specifics—what you want done, how much it's going to cost, and when it's going to be completed.

Americans spent more than $94 billion on home remodeling in 1987. Each job involved a legal contract, and many ended in problems: That year, according to the Better Business Bureau, 45,750 complaints were filed against home-improvement companies and contractors, making it the fourth-most-frequent kind of complaint lodged with the BBB. Most complaints were that the job wasn't finished on time or correctly. That's why it's so important that you have complete information about contractors and home-improvement agreements *before* starting a job.

A CASE STUDY

Connie and David Wade, of Sacramento, California, never dreamed when they hired a general contractor to oversee construction of their new home that so many problems could be caused by one person.

After they fired him, they filed papers listing a new general contractor's name with their title company. Too late, they discovered the title company could not record the new papers because a *mechanic's lien* for $125,000 had been filed against their property by the first contractor. This lien froze their construction loan until they paid what the contractor demanded.

Desperate, the Wades tried to get insurance to cover the lien. That required coming up with one-and-a-half times the amount of the lien in cash. They turned to the state's licensing board for help but found it had a three-month backlog. To free up money so construction could proceed, the Wades were forced to pay the shoddy contractor $5,000 in cash to dismiss the lien.

If the Wades had had correct information, they could have prevented the nightmare in a number of ways. The contractor could have been prosecuted for breach of contract if the Wades had thought to include written deadlines in their contract. Or, they could have required the contractor to sign a *lien waiver* form before each payment.

CONTRACTORS

Don't let the Wades' example frighten you. Many contractors are hardworking, honest, and talented tradespeople interested in doing good work. Their biggest motivation (as in any business) is making money. That's an important incentive, so if you're trying to get a sun deck installed for the cost of the materials alone, don't be surprised if no one's interested in the job.

Several types of contractors do home improvement work: general contractors, independent contractors, and subcontractors. Both general and independent contractors offer building services, and both are responsible for overseeing and being legally responsible for the entire project. The independent is in business alone, whereas general contractors may employ other contractors as well as sell their own services. Subcontractors are specialists hired to do specific tasks, such as electrical or plumbing work.

Before deciding to act as your own general contractor, you should know that you'll be undertaking a multitude of responsibilities:

- Buying supplies
- Obtaining permits
- Making sure renovations meet code or apartment building requirements
- Hiring and paying subcontractors
- Supervising the work

If something goes wrong, you, the general contractor, will be the one responsible. Make sure the money you save by not hiring a general contractor outweighs the headaches of being responsible for the work and the outcome of the project.

When should you act as the general contractor? It depends on the size and complexity of the job and how much free time you have. You can easily act as general contractor if the project is simple and won't take much time: installing a bay window, laying an oak floor, building a wall cabinet, or lowering a ceiling. If, however, you're authorizing a more complex home improvement—adding a room, for example—that requires hiring and working with a variety of people (carpenter, electrician, plasterer, and roofer), you'll need plenty of time and knowledge about how the improvement can best be done.

This chapter assumes you'll hire and work with an independent contractor.

INDEPENDENTS AND "SUBS"

Most people hire *independent contractors* to oversee the entire project, including drafting the work plans, hiring and paying subcontractors for specific tasks, arranging building permits and inspections, and providing workers' compensation and general liability insurance.

When you hire an independent, the contractor does not legally become your employee, and legal obligations normally imposed on employers do not apply. For example, you are not required to provide the contractor with workers' and unemployment compensation, tax withholding, or the like. Once given your instructions, the contractor has complete control to direct what, when, and how things are to be done. Your "control" is limited to approving the finished product.

You *are* legally responsible as an employer, however, if you hire someone from down the street to paint your house and that person doesn't maintain a separate business, relies on you for tools, works at your location, and is closely supervised by you. Such a worker is considered your employee under the law, so you would be legally responsible for insurance against job-related injuries.

A subcontractor, referred to in the trade as a *sub,* is a specialist hired by an independent contractor to do a specific job or jobs on your home improvement. Electricians, plumbers, plasterers, drywall contractors, and painters are examples.

BASIC CONCEPTS

Qualifications

The most important qualification to consider when shopping for a contractor is experience. If you're having a bathroom installed, try to find someone who has experience with the kinds of work involved—plumbing, tiling, and the like. Many people in this field are "jacks-of-all-trades" and can competently handle a variety of home improvements, but you'll probably get what you want done more quickly and with less trouble if you hire someone who has demonstrated an ability in the area you need.

The *legal* qualifications for being a contractor vary. The contractor you hire may be licensed, certified, registered, or none of these. It all depends on where you live. According to a 1988 study by the National Association of Home Builders (NAHB), 22 states have licensing requirements for home remodelers, and nearly all states license electricians and plumbers. Getting a license in most states requires a specific amount of work experience and passing an exam. The licensing requirements in California, Florida, and Maryland are among the nation's most stringent.

Seven states (Arkansas, Connecticut, Georgia, Kansas, Nebraska, New Jersey, and West Virginia) have *registration* requirements for home remodelers. To register, contractors simply file their name and address with the appropriate state agency before practicing their trade. They may also have to pay a registration fee, but nothing else is required.

A few states also have certification, in addition to licensing. The certification program is designed for those who want special recognition for their skill. It requires passing another exam and paying yet another fee.

If you're having extensive work done, using a licensed contractor can have three advantages. First, a licensed contractor typically is required to carry insurance. This protects you if your property is damaged or the people working on it are injured. Second, many licensed contractors belong to trade associations that can help you settle disputes or disagreements if they arise. Finally, a licensed contractor may be more willing than someone else to try to resolve problems, especially if the license is at stake.

For information on the licensing requirements in your state, contact your state's licensing agency, usually called the Contractors Licensing Board, or the State Licensing Board for General Contractors.

Bonds

Most states require licensed contractors to be bonded. A *bond* is insurance that compensates you, up to a certain amount, for shoddy work by a contractor. If contractors aren't required to be licensed or registered in your state, it's particularly important to make sure they're bonded. Ask to see their insurance papers. If the contractor you're hiring balks at that request, be wary. Good contractors can find insurance easily and quickly.

A *surety* or *performance bond* issued by an insurance company guarantees that if the contractor goes bankrupt or otherwise fails to live up to the contract, any money owed to you, subcontractors, or suppliers will be taken care of, up to a specified limit.

Find out what the bond covers and for how much before

hiring a contractor. Some bonds protect you only against substandard work that doesn't comply with the building code. As a result, you may have to live with work that doesn't violate the code but is shoddy nonetheless.

Permits, Codes, and Inspections

A *building permit* is required when structural work is involved or a home's basic living area is to be changed. For example, if you're turning a garage into a family room or an attic into a bedroom, you need a building permit because you're changing the amount of "livable" space in your home. By getting a building permit, you notify the city or county of your project, allowing the building inspector to schedule *inspections* throughout the course of construction to make sure it meets code requirements. All contractors should know state and local requirements for *building permits, inspections,* and *codes.*

The contractor should obtain the necessary permit from your town or county Building Inspector's Office before beginning work. Whoever applies for the building permit is the one ultimately responsible if the work doesn't comply with building codes, so unless you've taken on the responsibility as general contractor, let the contractor apply for the permit. The contractor must display the permit in a public area. The cost of permits and inspections is usually included in the contractor's bid.

Obtaining a *building permit* is usually not difficult, unless your plans encroach on someone else's property or violate your local government's zoning regulations. It's the contractor's responsibility to notify the inspector when the job is at the half or three-quarter point, the stages when inspections are usually done.

Building codes set minimum safety standards. Remember that a contractor can meet these minimum safety requirements and still botch the appearance of the final job. You can get a copy of the code at your town hall.

Mechanic's Lien

If you don't pay contractors, subcontractors, or suppliers, state laws allow them to place a *mechanic's lien* on your property, giving them the right to sell it to pay the debt owed them.

Even if you've paid in full, the subcontractors and suppliers can file a mechanic's lien against your home if they haven't been paid by your general contractor. Unfair as it seems, this could force you to pay your bill twice. To protect yourself, ask the general contractor to provide proof that workers and suppliers are being paid with each installment and include a *release of lien* in your contract. This puts all workers and suppliers on notice that, before receiving payment, they will have to sign a lien *waiver* form. The waiver states that they cannot place a lien on your property if they've accepted payment. Ask your contractor for a waiver form.

To protect yourself further from liens by subcontractors and suppliers, make your payments jointly payable. Write a check to both the contractor and supplier, or to both the contractor and the sub. That way, all parties involved will have to endorse your check.

Late or Poor Work

Delays occur for many reasons: unavailable materials, weather problems, absent subs. Delays can also occur if your contractor doesn't take the job seriously or isn't told when certain stages of the construction are expected to be completed.

All home improvement contracts should state specific deadlines for completion. For example: foundation in by August 2, framing by September 3, and roofing by November 25. In addition, if you're concerned about a contractor falling behind schedule, include a provision that *"time is of the essence."* This language is primarily used when timing is critical—for example, getting the roof on your house before the rainy season.

"Time is of the essence" is a legal phrase interpreted by courts to mean that completion dates are important to you. If the contractor is late, you can be compensated either by having your bill reduced each day the job is not done or by requiring the contractor to pay for damages caused by the lateness. Damage done to your hardwood floor by rain that came through the incomplete roof repair is one example.

The best protection you can get against poor or incomplete work is by spelling out in your contract your right to inspect the work before you make the final payment.

If the contractor disagrees with you about the quality of the work, a court will determine whether the contractor complied with the material terms of the contract. If a judge or arbitrator decides that the contractor did comply, you'll be ordered to pay the balance due on the contract, perhaps minus a reasonable amount you'll need to hire someone to complete work not done to your satisfaction. If it's ruled that the contractor didn't live up to the contracted terms, you'll probably owe nothing more.

Environmental Toxins

State and federal laws regulate the detection, treatment, and removal of environmental toxins, such as asbestos fibers and lead paint. Contractors are required to obtain special licenses and permits before handling these substances.

Today, many contractors are including in their contracts language that releases them from liability for refusing to work with or to be exposed to toxins. Before signing a contract that has such a provision, ask the contractor to investigate and test the premises for hazardous substances. Contractors are required by law to provide this service free. If toxic substances are detected, you can decide how to proceed and make sure your contractor has the proper qualifications to handle them.

CHAPTER 9

BEFORE YOU SIGN

Before hiring a contractor and agreeing on what will be done and for how much, you need to prepare yourself with some preliminary decisions.

Know What You Want Done

To get the most satisfactory results, take an active role in the project. It's not enough to say you want the kitchen remodeled without giving the contractor your ideas on layout, design, and materials. For example, offer ideas about:

- The size of the kitchen
- Placement of doors and windows
- Size and placement of cabinets
- Placement of stove, sink, and refrigerator
- Tile, Formica, or other surface materials
- Built-in cutting boards, lazy Susan, or microwave shelf
- Electrical and plumbing needs
- Wall coverings, moldings, or ceiling beams

When you know what you want done and exactly what's involved to complete the work, you can make better decisions about hiring and how to achieve the home improvements with minimum disruption of your family, lifestyle, and pocketbook.

Establish a Budget

Knowing how much you can afford will help you decide the size and quality of the project. Before talking to contractors, estimate how much you want to spend.

This helps potential contractors calculate how best to meet your budget requirements. If most contractors can't meet your budget without cutting corners or using cheap materials, you may have to scale down the size of the renovation or rethink the project entirely.

Find Financing

If you own a home, condo, co-op, or an apartment building, you can finance improvements in a number of ways. The best for you depends on how much money you need and how quickly the work has to be done. A common way is through bank or credit union loans. *Construction loans* (money specifically lent to finance a building project) are offered by most lending institutions (see Chapter 5).

When you apply for a loan, ask for 10% to 20% more than the contractor estimated the job will cost. If the money runs out before the project is complete, you may not have time to refinance. You'll avoid the headaches later by giving the bank a high estimate now.

You may be eligible for a Federal Housing Administration (FHA) loan insured through the U.S. Department of Housing and Urban Development (HUD). HUD offers a variety of home-improvement loans, including an FHA Title 1 loan of up to $17,500 (in 1989) for any home improvement that makes a single-family unit, individual condo or co-op, or apartment unit you own more livable or useful. Several restrictions apply, however. For example, you can't use the money to buy luxury items like swimming pools or saunas or to improve the outside of a condominium or co-op building. You can, however, install a dishwasher, refrigerator, built-in oven, and the like to improve the quality of your living environment. For more information on Title 1 and other FHA loans, contact a HUD regional office (Appendix IV).

Although more difficult to find, some cities and counties offer one-time home improvement *grants* to people who want to renovate homes in certain neighborhoods. These grants do not have to be paid back. If grants are available in your area, the Mayor's or City Council Office should be able to tell you how to apply.

Prepare Work Plans, Specifications

The *work plans* and *specifications* explain in words and drawings the measurements and materials to be used in your renovation. They also show how the project will look when it's finished. Typically, the contractor or an architect draws up the plans. You can, however, provide ideas about what you want done by giving contractors an initial sketch. Don't worry if your sketch is not to scale. You'll probably give a much better idea of what you want done with a drawing than you can with only words, regardless of how amateurish the drawing is. In turn, the contractor can add suggestions or make corrections and give you a detailed drawing done to scale.

If you don't feel comfortable about drawing your own plans, make sure you check the contractor's or architect's draft design. Don't hand over the entire project with a "talk to me when it's over" attitude, unless you're willing to take virtually any result you get.

For specific design suggestions or ideas, check home-improvement books and magazines available in most bookstores. Magazines, in particular, can keep you up to date on the latest in materials, designs, and building techniques.

HIRING A CONTRACTOR

Shopping

The best way to find a reliable and competent contractor is to do comparative shopping. Ask for recommendations from people who have already had similar work done. Also, get names of reliable contractors from people who frequently do business with them: bankers, supply stores, trade associations, and local building inspectors.

Although you must carefully check advertised facts, the Yellow Pages or the advertisement section of a local newspaper can also put you in touch with qualified contractors.

Before considering an unsolicited contractor, check references and ask about the contractor's license, bond, and trade-association membership, if any. Then, if you think it's necessary, get a second or even third opinion on the repairs the soliciting contractor is suggesting. Above all, don't rush into anything.

Sometimes contractors will come looking for you. Some who do this are disreputable and cheat homeowners out of thousands of dollars each year. A common tactic is to convince victims that their homes need unnecessary repairs—a new roof, gutter, or paint job.

A Case Study

Two dishonest contractors, brothers, recently bilked more than $300,000 from Katherine Fink, a 77-year-old resident of Baltimore, Maryland. Among other charges, she was billed $6,000 to replace a toilet, $9,000 to replace a kitchen radiator, and $8,000 each for five other radiators in her house. The contractors splashed water on the walls and floors to convince her that repairs were needed to avoid water damage. They also pulled out electrical wires that were in perfect condition and punched a hole in the pipe leading to her gas range to create yet more work. Their licenses were later suspended. Ms. Fink, who was able to recover only $20,000 from a Guarantee Fund of the Maryland Home Improvement Commission, now faces years of litigation to try to collect the rest of her loss.

The Interview

Whether you find them or they find you, you should interview at least three contractors if yours is a large job. If you need to scale down your list, do it by making a few telephone calls first. You can easily eliminate some names over the telephone: Some won't be taking on additional work, others won't be available when you need them, and still others won't be in your price range.

When you've narrowed your list, it's time to set up in-person interviews. You need to know the contractor's training and experience, how much you'll be charged, and how long the project will take. The contractor can supply you with time and cost estimates in writing after getting the chance to look over the place you want renovated or the space you want added onto.

Before the interview, send all contractors the same information about the project, your budget, and any work sketches you have. Some questions to ask at the interview:

When Did You Get Into This Business? How Many Jobs Do You Have Going? What Type of Remodeling Work Do You Typically Do?   Answers to these questions will help you determine if this is someone you want to hire. A person who has only a few jobs going may just be starting out and willing to charge less. Someone who is extremely busy might be a good catch but hard to hold.

Are You Licensed and Bonded?   Not all states require this, but if they do, ask to see the license and get the license number, then check to see if the license is current. Consider checking the contractor's status with the state's licensing board. Also, ask the bonding company what the bond covers and what its maximum payout is.

Do You Belong to a Trade Association?   If the answer is yes, ask which one, and call to make sure the membership is current. Two of the largest trade associations are the Remodelers Council of the National Association of Home Builders (NAHB) and the National Association of the Remodeling Industry (NARI). Both promote the professional remodeling and rehabilitation industries, providing their members business and technical support.

If your contractor belongs to such an association, ask if it will act as intermediary between you and the contractor if things go wrong.

Do You Carry Liability and Workers' Compensation Insurance?   This insurance protects you, your neighbors, passers-by, and all workers in case of an accident. Ask to see Certificates of Insurance or check coverage by asking the contractor's insurance carrier.

Is There a Warranty on Your Work? Materials? For How Long?   Make sure you get all warranties in writing. A warranty is a promise or guarantee by the contractor or manufacturer of the supplier's products to stand behind its service or product if something goes wrong.

Ask if the quality of both the work and the materials is covered by warranty, and who will make good on it if there's trouble. How long is the warranty good for? Is it a *full* or *limited* warranty? If it's a full warranty, all products found to be faulty will have to be repaired or replaced or your full purchase price will be refunded. If it's a limited warranty, some limitations will apply on the repair or replacement. Ask what these are.

Will You Put Your Fees in Writing?   The law requires that contracts that involve more than $500 must be in writing. That includes home-improvement contracts. Once signed, the contract cannot be changed unless otherwise provided for in the contract itself or unless you approve the changes.

Are You Willing to Be Paid in Installments and to Accept Final Payment Only after the Job Is Completed by the Terms of Our Agreement?   It's common practice to reserve 10% or more of the fee to be paid only after you and a local government inspector have examined the work and you've signed a certificate of completion.

If during the interview the contractor is difficult to talk to or uses language you don't understand, chances are communication will get worse once construction starts. You need to feel comfortable and confident about both the contractor's skills and personality. After all, if major repairs are planned, the contractor may be in your home for weeks or months.

Ask the contractor to supply you with a bid (a written estimate of how much materials and labor will cost) as soon as possible after the interview.

Evaluating Bids

Make sure each bid is based on the same work and includes the same-quality materials. A contractor who is under the impression you want custom-designed or imported materials is obviously going to quote you a higher bid than the one who gives you an estimate on less expensive materials. A contractor's bid should include:

- A description of the work to be done
- Approximate starting and completion dates
- The estimated cost of materials, labor, and building permits

The "quoted" bid is usually good for 30 days. Some contractors will submit a bid on a preprinted form that becomes your contract if you agree to it. These forms have contract language that tends to favor the contractor, much as pre-printed leases favor landlords. If you plan to accept a bid, make sure you read the fine print and understand everything in it before signing. Once signed, it's a legally enforceable contract. If you think it's necessary, ask to make changes and to add or strike provisions. Be sure to check our translations and advice in the next chapter.

Initial any changes you make on the preprinted form. If the contractor doesn't agree to them, find someone who will. Remember, you can accept the estimate but do not have to accept the contract it's written on. You can use a different form or write your own. As long as you're reasonable and not expecting the contractor to work for nothing, the contractor shouldn't mind drafting a contract that meets with your approval.

References

Ask the contractors you're most interested in to give you the names of past clients and suppliers. When you've narrowed your choices, you'll have several more ways to measure them. You can check firsthand the quality of their finished work by visiting past clients, and you can see if they pay bills on time by checking with their suppliers. A third check is to ask the Better Business Bureau or your local Office of Consumer Affairs if any complaints have been registered against the contractor. Both organizations usually will let you know.

In 1987 alone, the Better Business Bureau received 897,600 requests for information about home-improvement companies and contractors. Take advantage of the information they collect by calling the bureau nearest you. They're listed in Appendix II.

Making Payments

The amount you pay the contractor at any given stage is also important. You want to give enough money so work can proceed but not so much that the contractor doesn't have a continuing incentive to finish the job. With minor jobs, a small deposit upon signing the contract or after materials are bought is typical, with the balance paid upon completion.

Large home improvements will require several installments. You and the contractor may have conflicting interests here. You will want to make payments as stages are completed, while the contractor will want money before stages are begun. The best way to get around this is to start with a reasonable deposit of 10% to 20%, smaller payments during construction, and slightly less than half (about 40%) upon completion. Being owed a substantial part of the money near the end gives the contractor incentive to finish. Make sure you do not make your final payment until the project is completed, the releases of liens are signed and handed in by subs and suppliers, the building authorities have completed their inspections satisfactorily, and all warranties are in your hands: Then and only then should you sign the last check.

CHAPTER 10

SOLVING PROBLEMS

This section briefly describes your options for resolving disputes with home-improvement contractors and should be read with the general problem-solving information in Chapter 4. A well-written contract will prevent misunderstandings and help you resolve disputes through direct negotiation. However, if attempts at negotiation fail, several agencies may be able to help you resolve your problem at little or no expense.

Licensing Authorities

If your contractor is licensed, start by contacting the licensing authority. This agency keeps current records about work and home addresses of its contractors and will be able to track yours down more easily. Also, you can usually get the agency to investigate your complaint and, if applicable, forward it to the bonding company. Getting a bonding company to pay up on a claim is not always easy, unless the contractor readily admits guilt. Otherwise, you'll have to prove the contractor's guilt, probably in court, before your claim will be paid.

The amount of help a state's licensing board will give varies. Some state agencies have authority not only to license contractors, but to investigate complaints and, if necessary, suspend or revoke their licenses.

At least one state, Maryland, goes a step further and requires contractors to pay $50 into a restitution fund used to reimburse victims of fraudulent or incompetent work. This is called the Guaranteed Fund of the Home Improvement Commission, operated by the Maryland Department of Licensing and Regulation. It holds hearings to determine if complaints are valid and then reimburses complainants up to $10,000 per homeowner or $50,000 per contractor. Consumers can receive as much as $2,500 from the fund without attending a hearing, more than that if they win their case in arbitration or receive a nondefault court judgment against the contractor.

Don't expect too much from licensing agencies, however. Many are criticized for siding with the construction industry in their decisions and for not being aggressive enough in compensating victimized consumers. Even Maryland's Guaranteed Fund has come under attack.

Trade Associations

If you're dealing with a licensed contractor, chances are you're also dealing with someone who belongs to a trade association. If the licensing board in your area isn't helpful, try the contractor's trade association. Many, like the National Association of Home Builders (NAHB) and the National Association of the Remodeling Industry (NARI), will contact the contractor on your behalf to help resolve the dispute.

Consumer Affairs Offices, Better Business Bureaus

If you still can't get adequate help, the next step is to complain in writing to a government Consumer Affairs Office or Better Business Bureau. Both handle consumer complaints and, depending on the office, may specialize in dealing with complaints against contractors. (For more information on these agencies, see Chapter 4.)

Formal Dispute Resolution

If informal methods of resolving your dispute don't work, consider mediation, arbitration, or a lawsuit. All are discussed in Chapter 4. Be advised, however, that *construction* arbitration can sometimes be as expensive and complicated as litigation, especially if a lot of money is at stake. Expert testimony, witnesses, and thorough documentation will probably be required.

The American Arbitration Association (AAA) is a private organization that offers arbitration of construction disputes. It requires lengthy application forms and a filing fee—up to 3% of the amount in the dispute, with a $300 minimum—to be paid before arbitration begins.

Explore all your arbitration alternatives if you go this route. Some jurisdictions may offer court-annexed arbitration, and that may be less expensive than the AAA's services. Ask at your local court clerk's office.

RESOURCES

For more information, contractor referrals, and sample home-improvement contracts, contact the following trade associations:

American Homeowners
Foundation
1724 S. Quincy St.
Arlington, VA 22205

National Association of the
Remodeling Industry
1901 N. Moore St., Suite 808
Arlington, VA 22209

Remodelers Council of the
National Association of Home
Builders
15th and M Sts. NW
Washington, DC 20005

Home Owner's Warranty
Corporation (HOW)
2000 L St. NW
Washington, DC 20036

American Institute of Architects
1735 New York Ave. NW
Washington, DC 20006

The following free brochures, of five to 10 pages each, offer advice on shopping for a contractor, writing contracts, and getting help with problems.

Choosing a Professional Remodeling Contractor. Prepared by U.S. Office of Consumer Affairs, Better Business Bureau, the National Association of Consumer Agency Administrators and the Remodelers Council of the National Association of Home Builders.

Home Help: How to Get It & Who Can Do It. My Home Magazine Referral Network, 6715 Lowell Ave., Suite 2, McLean, VA 22101.

Home Improvements and Repairs. Wisconsin Department of Justice, Office of Consumer Protection, 123 W. Washington Ave., Madison, WI 53707.

How to Choose a Remodeler Who's on the Level. Send self-addressed, stamped envelope to the Remodelers Council of the National Association of Home Builders at the address above.

Selecting a Professional Remodeling Contractor. National Association of the Remodeling Industry (address above).

Simple Home Repairs Inside. Consumer Information Center—E, P.O. Box 100, Pueblo, CO 81002.

Tips on Home Improvements. Better Business Bureau, 1515 Wilson Blvd., Arlington, VA 22209.

CHAPTER 11

CONTRACT LANGUAGE

For your protection, your agreement with your contractor should be in writing. It should describe the job the contractor is to complete, the materials to be used, the total price, and the payment schedule. Your contract should also include a provision for arbitration of unforeseen disputes.

If you authorize home improvements without a written agreement, or if you simply sign a preprinted bid from the contractor, you run the risk of costly mistakes.

You have several options: You can use a standard building-contract form and modify it to fit the work you want done; you can revise the contractor's suggested contract; or you can write your own.

Writing your own contract for simple home improvements is not difficult, though the contractor is certain to scrutinize it before signing. To avoid disagreements, discuss major provisions you want to include with the contractor in advance—for example, provisions for making payments, approving work, storing equipment, or settling disputes.

If you don't feel comfortable writing your own contract and don't want to pay a lawyer to do it for you, think about using a preprinted form. Such forms, complete with instructions, are offered by several building-trade associations, including those listed at the end of Chapter 10.

In this chapter, we've drafted a pro-consumer agreement that contains the most important elements of a home improvement contract. For additional items, you may wish to consult page 106, Other Important Clauses.

HOME IMPROVEMENT CONTRACT

On this, the _____ day of _____, 19___,
_____ (Owner)
residing at _____
and_____ (Contractor)
doing business at _____
agree as follows:

1. Work to Be Performed.
   At the following address,_____
   _____contractor will:_____
   _____
   _____

   _____. For a detailed description of the work involved, parties will refer to the attached drawings and specifications which are incorporated into this agreement by this reference.

First, fill in the date, your name and address, and the name and address of the contractor.

In Clause 1, in the space provided, you should note a brief description of your project—basement refinishing, room addition, kitchen remodeling, etc.—and the address of the property to be remodeled.

The "drawings and specifications" are the *work plans* discussed in Chapter 9. They are the illustrations and written instructions of your project and are an important part of every home improvement agreement. If a disagreement arises over materials, labor, or design, you'll need to refer to these drawings and specifications for direction, so make sure they are specific, accurate, and attached to this document.

2. Starting and Completion Dates.
   The contractor shall start work on _____, 19___ and subject

to authorized time adjustments, complete work no later than
_____, 19___.

A clause explaining when work is to begin and when it must be completed is extremely important. Many home-improvement contracts state when a project is to begin but not when it is to be finished. If a final date is missing from the contract you receive, make sure it's added. This is the date when *all* the work, without exception, must be finished.

3. Date of Substantial Completion.
   Work will be substantially completed, subject to authorized time adjustments, on _____, 19___.

   If work is not substantially completed by _____, 19___, contractor will owe owner $___ for each day beyond the date of substantial completion.

In this clause, insert the date by which most of the work (substantial completion) should be done. Although not defined, substantial completion is considered the point at which the space or area can be used for its intended purpose. Dates when other phases of the work have to be completed, if necessary, can be written into a separate clause (see page 109, Time Is of the Essence).

A provision that will compensate you if the contractor fails to meet the substantial completion date is important. You and the contractor should agree upon a "good faith" estimate of how much you will get if the contractor is late.

Some contracts actually list what the amount will be, for example, $50 or $100 per day. If you get such a contract and do not agree with the stated penalty amount, try to get the contractor to change it before you sign. If you don't and a dispute later ensues, a court or arbitrator (depending on what your contract states about resolving disputes) will decide what a reasonable estimate should have been at the time the contract was signed.

4. Price.
Owner agrees to pay contractor in cash, certified check or money order, a sum total of $_____, subject to authorized additions or deductions of that price.

This clause lists the total amount you'll pay (Price) for the entire project. That price may eventually go up or down depending on any changes you authorize once construction is under way. For example, if you change your mind and substitute a Superduper Deluxe washing machine for a Wash-O-Matic by Wring 'n' Rinse, the total price will probably increase. Or, if the contractor can't find the exact materials you requested and needs to use substitutes (as often happens), that will affect the total cost.

5. Schedule of Payments.
Owner agrees to reimburse contractor for the total cost of the contract, including labor, materials and equipment, upon receiving a written request for payment and a satisfactory work inspection, as follows:
10% payable upon signing of this contract.
15% payable after ____ weeks.
15% payable after ____ weeks.
20% payable upon date of substantial completion.
40% payable upon completion.

If a payment is not received within ____ days of being due, the owner shall pay contractor an additional ____% of the total amount overdue.

Paying the contractor in installments (or "draws," as progress payments are sometimes called in the construction business) is standard. Under this clause, two things need to occur before each payment will be made: The work has to pass inspection (by the town inspector or whomever you've chosen to conduct inspections) and the contractor has to provide you with a written request for payment.

To make sure you hold up your end of the bargain, a late

charge is assessed if you do not make payments within the time line given. You and the contractor must decide when payments are due and how much will be charged if they're late.

This clause also allows you to reserve 40% of the pay till the end. Some contractors may balk at this (and you may have to compromise), but leaving a substantial amount to be paid on completion helps to prevent contractors from leaving a job unfinished.

> 6. Final Payment.
> Final payment, the entire unpaid balance of the amount due, shall be paid by the owner to the contractor when the work has been completed, the contract has been fully performed, the work has passed inspection and the owner has given final approval.

Most home improvement contracts make final payment contingent on something. This one makes final payment contingent on the work being completed, passing inspection, and receiving final approval from you.

Allowing you to give final approval is *not* standard, and you will probably not see anything like it in a preprinted form. It is included here to give you leverage, within reason, but is not meant to give you an easy way out of paying what you owe. Contractors may allow you to write a contract or revise a final-payment provision in a way that gives you final approval, but they won't hesitate to take you to court if they think they've met their obligations but you haven't paid. If a judge or arbitrator has to decide this type of dispute, expect the doctrine of substantial performance to be used in determining whether or not you owe more money (see Glossary, Appendix V).

> 7. Acknowledgment of Payment and Waiver of Mechanic's Lien.
> The owner will require the contractor to attach to each

request for partial or final payment, an acknowledgment of payment, and all subcontractors' acknowledgments of payment, for work done and materials, equipment and fixtures furnished through the date covered by the previous payment. Concurrently with the final payment, the owner will require the contractor to execute a waiver or release of lien for all work performed and materials furnished hereunder and to obtain similar waivers or releases from all subcontractors and suppliers.

This is an important protection for you. It requires the contractor to give you a document called an Acknowledgment of Payment each time you make a payment for labor or materials, to serve as proof that your bills are being paid.

Each year, hundreds of consumers are cheated by contractors who don't pay their subcontractors or suppliers with the funds they've been entrusted with. This language prevents such abuse by also requiring contractors, subcontractors, and suppliers to sign a "waiver of mechanic's liens" before you make your final payment. If this waiver *isn't* signed and your contractor doesn't pay off the subs or suppliers, a mechanic's lien might be attached to your property and stop you from selling or mortgaging it, even though you've already paid the contractor.

Because you're ultimately responsible for all debts incurred, we strongly urge you to make *sure* this language is included in your home-improvement contract. Be aware, however, that many contract forms include language similar to this but use the word "may" instead of "will" ("The owner may require . . ."). The stronger, more definite language we suggest allows no room for misunderstanding. While some contractors may fuss about it, such language will certainly not be new to them.

8. Supplying Materials.
   The contractor shall provide all materials and equipment required to carry out the terms of the contract.

This language places responsibility on the contractor to supply all materials and all equipment needed to get the job done. It can be changed to fit your circumstances. For example, you may prefer that the contractor save you money by installing used parts. Or you may want to be responsible for buying the materials or supplying equipment if you believe you can save money that way.

9. Warranty.
The contractor warrants that all materials will be new unless otherwise specified, and that all materials will be of good quality and covered by manufacturers' warranties. The contractor will supply the owner with copies of all manufacturers' warranties. The contractor also warrants that the work, including work done by subcontractors, will be of good quality, free from faults and defects in workership for a period of _____ from the date the work is completed.

This requires the contractor to guarantee (warrant) that the materials are new and to give you copies of warranties for all materials covered by manufacturer's warranty. It also requires the contractor to guarantee the work for a specified time after the job is completed: If the work is found to be faulty (for example, if the toilet begins to leak) within the time specified, you can call the contractor back to correct the work without charge. You have the right to expect the contractor to guarantee work for a reasonable length of time. The current market standard is 12 months.

10. Change in Plans.
The owner, without invalidating the contract, may order changes in the work within the general scope of the contract consisting of additions, deletions or other revisions. The contract price and the contract time will be adjusted accordingly. All such changes in the work shall be in writing, and signed by the contractor and owner and attached to this document.

Change orders (sometimes referred to as "addenda" or "modifications") are papers that specify changes you authorize in the original agreement before or after work has started. For example, if the agreed-upon completion date has to be pushed back because of inclement weather, draft a change order that states the new date. It should be dated and signed by you and the contractor. Once signed, change orders become official parts of your agreement and should be attached to it. If you're having a large job done, adding a room or remodeling a kitchen, for example, expect a number of change orders.

Change orders typically include:

- The name of the project (e.g., refinishing basement)
- The date of the change
- A precise description of the change
- A detailed description of necessary materials, including brand names
- Additional charges or deductions caused by the change
- Deadline changes
- Signatures of both the contractor and you

11. Noise, Cleanup, Storing Equipment.
The contractor at all times shall keep the premises free from accumulation of waste materials or rubbish caused by the operations. At the completion of the work each day, the contractor shall remove all waste materials and rubbish from and about the project and store all construction equipment, machinery and surplus materials.

If the contractor fails to clean up or store equipment at the completion of work each day, the owner may do so and be credited $_____ against the contract price for each day the owner takes care of cleanup.

To prevent neighbors from being unduly bothered by construction noise, contractor agrees to perform work between the hours of _____ A.M. and _____ P.M., on the following days of the week: _____.

Spelling out who will clean up and store equipment is especially important to include in your contract when large renovations are being done. It ensures that the work area is clean and safe at the end of each day. If you need the contractor to haul away large volumes of debris or large items like a refrigerator during or at the end of construction, you can expect to be charged extra for that.

A good "cleanup" credit you can ask for is $25 for each day you have to clear away debris or put away the contractor's tools and equipment. Disruptions cannot be entirely prevented, but they can be reduced.

Days of the week and hours of work should be spelled out, particularly because some communities have specific regulations about this. Specify "Monday through Friday only," if that is the agreement.

12. Arbitration.
    All claims, disputes and other matters in question between the contractor and owner arising out of or relating to the contract documents or the breach thereof, and not resolved by referring to the contract documents, shall be decided by arbitration in accordance with the construction industry arbitration rules of the American Arbitration Association, unless the parties mutually agree to resolve the dispute otherwise.

Arbitration clauses are common in consumer contracts. If you don't have such a provision, you run the risk of having to settle disputes in court, and that can be time-consuming and expensive. In arbitration, it's simple, less expensive, and quicker: You and the contractor meet with a neutral third party who listens to your testimony, reviews the evidence, and renders a final and binding decision.

This language suggests that your dispute be decided by an American Arbitration Association (AAA) arbitrator. AAA has been arbitrating construction disputes for years. However, the organization, a private corporation based in New York, has been criticized by some as pro-business. If you decide to use AAA, find out what arbitrator will be assigned your case, get a copy of the rules, and go into the meeting prepared with documented evidence of work plans, schedules, drawings, payments, photographs of the work in question, and any other pertinent materials. If you prefer, rewrite the contract language in the clause we've suggested by using the name of a different dispute resolution company or agency. Always check qualifications of the companies and individuals offering arbitration. You can find some in the telephone directory's Yellow Pages.

Owner	Contractor
Date: _____	Date: _____

Make sure to sign the contract, date it, and see that the contractor does the same.

OTHER IMPORTANT CLAUSES

The following provisions from a variety of other home-improvement contracts cover some of the other pro-consumer clauses a home-improvement contract could include.

RELATIONSHIP OF PARTIES

The parties intend that an independent contractor-owner relationship will be created by this contract. Owner is interested only in the results to be achieved. The conduct and control of the work will lie solely with contractor. It is understood that contractor is free to perform similar services for other customers while under contract with owner.

An independent contractor may use language like this to explain how your relationship with the contractor is to be conducted, though usually it is taken as "a given" and is not written in.

Legally, independent contractors have complete control over how the work is to be done. They make decisions about process, what tools to use, and how to do the work. They also hire and pay subcontractors, unless otherwise specified in your contract. (See Chapter 8 for the legal differences between "independent contractors" and "employees.") One way to make sure you don't lose total control of what's happening in your home is to substitute the following clause when you find this "Relationship of Parties" language in a contract you've been offered:

OWNER'S RIGHT OF SUPERVISION AND INSPECTION

In the performance of the work described in the contract, contractor is an independent contractor with the authority to control and direct the performance of the details of the work, owner being interested only in the results obtained. However, the work contemplated herein must meet the approval of owner and will be subject to owner's general right of inspection and supervision to secure his or her complete satisfaction.

You may or may not find this language in your home-improvement agreement. It makes two important points: that the independent contractor has total control over how the project will be done and that the finished product must get your approval.

This clause does not give you any new rights; it simply reinforces your right to stay involved, to inspect the work, and to offer comments if you think something should be done differently. Your right is limited to inspections and comments. The contractor is free to accept or reject your suggestions, but is reminded here that the work must get your approval, so it's probably wise to listen to you.

SUBCONTRACTORS

All or any portion of the work covered by this contract may be subcontracted by contractor, but any subcontract shall specify that there will be no contractual relationship between the owner and subcontractors, nor will the subcontracting of all or any portion of the work in any way relieve contractor of obligations to the owner under this contract.

This makes it clear that your independent contractor is solely responsible for hiring, supervising, and paying all subcontractors—electricians, plumbers, and carpenters, for example. If problems occur with a sub, the independent contractor will be responsible for settling it—for example, by firing a sub who consistently fails to report to work on time. The contractor cannot use the behavior or performance of a sub as an excuse for not fulfilling contract obligations to you, nor can the contractor involve you in any agreement she or he has with the sub.

Although independent contractors automatically assume responsibility over subs, your contract should include language that makes this clear. If you want the responsibility of hiring, supervising, and paying subs, substitute this language:

All or any part of the work covered by this contract may be subcontracted by owner. Owner will assume responsibility for hiring, paying and supervising subcontractors.

or

All or any part of the work covered by this contract may be subcontracted by owner. Owner will assume responsibility for hiring and paying subcontractors but contractor will assume responsibility for their supervision.

INDEMNITY OF OWNER

All work under this contract will be performed entirely at contractor's risk, and contractor assumes all responsibility for the condition of tools and equipment used in its performance. Contractor will carry, for the duration of this contract, general liability insurance in an amount acceptable to the owner. Contractor agrees to indemnify owner for any and all liability or loss arising in any way out of the performance of this contract.

This gives the contractor the responsibility of dealing with all injuries to people or property from the performance of the contract. It also requires the contractor to carry liability insurance to cover any claims that are made because of those injuries. (This does not apply to workers on the job, however, as they are covered under workers' compensation provisions.)

It makes sense to select a contractor who carries liability insurance. It's especially important, however, if you're having extensive repairs or renovations done. Say, for example, that a neighbor visits your house while it's under construction and is injured by a falling brick. If your contractor doesn't carry liability insurance, paying for your neighbor's injury will have to come out of your pocket or from your homeowner's insurance. If the contractor carries liability insurance, however, your neighbor could file directly with the contractor's insurance company.

TIME IS OF THE ESSENCE

Contractor is notified that time is of the essence and will make every effort to complete the job by the agreed-upon completion date. If most of the work is substantially completed by the agreed-upon date, that is cause enough for owner to continue making payments.

Delays, however, will be considered a serious breach, allowing the owner to be compensated as provided for in Clause 3.

If you have a specific and demonstrable reason to need work done by a certain date, include this language. For instance, say your basement floods easily and you need work done before the rainy season begins. Include language stating the importance of having the job completed on time. This language works, however, only if you have a clause that specifically states when the work is to be finished.

Also, if you include this clause without a good reason, a court is not likely to enforce it. If a court does enforce a time-is-of-the-essence clause, you will be compensated for the delays according to your substantial completion date provisions (see Clause 3).

TERMINATION

Contractor may end this contract if, through no fault of the contractor, the owner fails to make payments according to the time provisions stipulated in this contract. All disagreements over payments due and owing will be resolved in arbitration as provided for in Clause 12.

Owner may end this contract if the contractor's work is unsatisfactory. All disagreements over payments due and owing will be resolved in arbitration as provided for in Clause 12.

A provision like this, allowing either side to break the contract, appears in many home-improvement agreements. This one allows the contractor to stop work if the owner fails to meet the deadlines set by the "schedule of payments" provision. Other contracts include language even less hospitable to consumers, allowing the contractor to get out of his or her obligations if the work is stopped through no fault of the contractor's (e.g., a court order, or inclement weather that lasts 30 or more days). In the sample provision, if the contractor ends the agreement, he or she will have to turn to arbitration to resolve the money disputes that led to the termination of the contract.

The second paragraph turns the tables: It allows you to

break the agreement if the contractor doesn't do the work or fails to do it correctly. Again, disputes between you and the contractor will have to be resolved through arbitration.

PROTECTION FROM WEATHER

Contractor will take special precaution to protect work during inclement weather. No mortar, concrete, plaster, paint and the like shall be used during inclement weather unless proper and special precaution is taken to prevent damage. Contractor will also provide protective coverings.

If your project might be exposed to and damaged by bad weather, include this language. Contractors do not usually mind taking these extra precautions, because they'll require you to pay for any extra work or materials they need to fulfill the obligation.

Getting Out of a Contract

If you sign a contract and then realize you've made a mistake, don't panic. The Federal Trade Commission requires contractors to give you a cancellation form, sometimes called "A Right of Rescission Notice," at the time the contract is signed. It gives you the right to cancel the contract within three days of signing it. If you don't get such a form, ask the contractor for it or add such a statement to the end of your contract.

PART IV

REPAIRING
YOUR CAR

CHAPTER 12

AUTO REPAIRS

Dick dropped off his car for a tune-up and oil change. The mechanic gave an oral estimate of $89.95 and told him to pick up his car after 5:00 P.M. When he arrived to get the car, he found his bill exceeded the estimate by $50.

On a friend's advice, Pam marked the parts in her car that needed to be replaced: the tailpipe, muffler, and radiator. When the work was completed, she found that the radiator hadn't been replaced, even though she had been charged for it.

Debbie is proud of her ability as a backyard mechanic, but when her attempt to fix the carburetor failed, she decided to take her car to a nearby garage. The mechanic later called to suggest an engine overhaul. Debbie agreed without hesitating.

All three instances above involved auto repair contracts and the special rules that govern them. Getting your car repaired shouldn't be a traumatic experience, but for many of us it is. According to the Council of Better Business Bureaus, 28,100 complaints were filed with its affiliate offices against auto repair shops in 1987, ranking that group fifth nationally. In reality, the problem is even larger: In California alone, during the 1987–88 fiscal year, 25,367 complaints were registered with the Bureau of Automotive Repair in the State Department of Consumer Affairs.

LEGAL CONSIDERATIONS

The most frequent complaints against auto repair shops are those alleging charges for unnecessary repairs and repairs that were never done; used parts sold as new; and advertised "specials" that resulted in more expensive repairs.

A typical scam, confirmed by the California bureau, is a repair shop's suggestion that an engine overhaul is needed when the car already has a perfectly good engine. Never intending to do the work suggested, the shop simply steam-cleans the existing engine and spray-paints it to look new. The cost to the garage is minimal, but the customer winds up paying about $1,000.

Regulation

Less than a dozen states have laws that require licensing of auto-repair shops. According to the most recent study by the Automotive Parts and Accessories Association (APAA), by 1982 only six states (California, Connecticut, Hawaii, Michigan, New York, and Rhode Island) and the District of Columbia had laws that required licensing of repair shops. The agency responsible for licensing these shops varies from state to state, but in most it's the Attorney General's Office, the Department of Motor Vehicles (DMV), or the Office of Consumer Affairs. The kind of help you may get from these agencies varies and is described in Chapter 4.

Disclosure Laws

More than half the states and the District of Columbia have "truth in auto repair" or "good-faith disclosure" laws. Such laws require repair shops to give consumers written estimates, to notify them in advance if the estimate will be exceeded, to return replaced parts, and to itemize repair bills, stating whether the parts installed were used, new, or repaired.

Disclosure laws vary. In Maryland, written estimates are required only on repairs that exceed $50, and a customer can be charged up to 10% more than the estimate without being contacted in advance. In California, however, customers must get written estimates on *all* repairs before any work is done; they cannot be charged more than the estimate unless they have approved the charge in advance.

The best way to protect yourself is to know what the laws are in your state. For more information, call your local or state Office of Consumer Affairs (Appendix I). Most of these offices offer basic advice and distribute pamphlets that describe your state's laws regulating auto repairs.

Lemon Laws

New-car owners who find themselves with unexpected and numerous repair bills can also find help. As of 1989, 45 states and the District of Columbia have *lemon laws* that require manufacturers to make their cars conform to warranty within a prescribed time or replace the vehicle entirely. These are described in Chapter 13.

Armed with correct information, you should be able to get competent, quality auto care without being overcharged. This and the next two chapters describe auto repair shops, offering advice on how to find a good one; what to look for in a mechanic; how to review a "repair order"; and your options if something goes wrong.

REPAIR SHOPS

Where you go depends on what you need done, your budget, the kind of personal service you're accustomed to or want, and, of course, the location of the repair shop. Repair shops belong to national chains, new-car dealerships, and independent garages. Each has advantages and disadvantages.

Chains

Large discount department stores like Zayres, Sears, K mart, and Montgomery Ward now operate auto-service centers. They offer routine services, like muffler installation, batteries, tune-ups, oil changes, tire mountings, front-end alignments, and brake work. Discount chains offer both brand-name parts and lower-cost parts sold under their own house labels.

Tire Outlets

Tire manufacturers, such as Goodyear and Firestone, and tire stores, like Merchant's Tire and Auto Centers, have also entered the auto repair business. Their primary enterprise is selling tires, so they limit the type of repair services they offer, typically to computerized tire balancing, complete front-end alignment, disc and drum brake repairs, and shock absorbers. Some also work on radiators, battery installation, and air conditioners.

The major difference between tire manufacturers and tire stores is in the parts they sell. Tire manufacturers sell their own brand-name parts, and tire stores sell a variety of both brand names and discount parts.

Specialty Franchises

Nationwide companies, such as AAMCO Transmissions and Midas Muffler Shops, specialize in specific repairs—rebuilt transmissions, muffler installations, exhaust-system work. Despite their televised advertisement claims, however, these specialty franchises tend to charge as much as 20% or 30% more for their work than the market rate. In return, customers get a full guarantee on both parts and labor and can count on getting their cars back quickly.

Service Stations

Like the "garages" of yesteryear, service stations still offer a variety of services, from oil changes and tune-ups to major engine work. Some services are offered free to regular customers, for example, adding oil that you supply, checking your tires' pressure, or adding water to the radiator. Other service, if simple (taping a leaky hose, for instance), might be handled by a station attendant at a smaller cost than if the station's mechanic had to do it.

If personalized service is what you want, find a local station you like and use it whenever you have repair needs it can handle. Repeat customers get much better service in this shrinking market.

If your car needs heavier work done and your station's mechanic can't handle it, ask to be referred to an independent garage.

Dealerships

If your car is still under warranty, the dealer you bought it from is the best place to go. You may be able to get the repairs done free under the warranty. Also, the dealer will be familiar with the type of car and have most if not all the necessary parts in stock. If the repair you need is at all complex, the dealership may be the only place to take it.

On the other hand, if all you need is routine work not covered by your warranty, you can probably get a better deal outside. This is because dealerships' per-hour labor charges tend to be high to cover overhead. Once the new-car warranty expires, people seldom return to their dealership for minor repairs.

Independents

Taking your car to an independent garage can be the best or worst thing you do. If you don't do homework in advance to learn how a garage and its mechanics operate, you could be headed for trouble.

Like service stations and store chains, independents' services vary. Some work only on domestic cars, others handle both foreign and domestic. Mechanics who have expertise in more than one area (for example, with diesel or fuel-injection work) are common at these garages, and many of them carry or can get both new and rebuilt parts. Taking your car to an independent is not always possible, because in many localities garages are extremely busy, have more work than they can handle, and will often act as though they are doing you a great kindness to work on your car. If you live in such an area, the best course of action is to find a good repair shop, establish a relationship with the owner, and stick with the shop as long as the work and the prices are good.

Whether or not you are in this situation, it is best to shop first. The following sections' tips should help.

FINDING THE RIGHT SHOP

Once you've decided what type of repair shop you want, you need assurance that the one you pick offers competent work at reasonable prices. The best way to do that is with legwork. Ask for recommendations, interview shop operators by telephone, and make at least one visit to the shop.

Recommendations

Word of mouth is invaluable in this field. Try to get a referral from a satisfied customer, someone who's had good or consistent success with a particular shop or mechanic.

In the unlikely event you can find no one who can tell you about experiences using the shop you're considering, ask your local Better Business Bureau or government Consumer Affairs Office. Both can tell you if any complaints have been received against the shop you're considering and what those complaints were about.

If you're a member of the American Automobile Association (AAA), call there for a referral as well, but be aware that the garage it refers you to will probably be one the AAA has "approved" or is in some way associated with. You'll have no guarantee of getting the best price available, but at least you'll have the AAA to complain to if trouble develops.

Visit and Ask Questions

If yours isn't an emergency or rush job, it makes sense to visit the shop first, look around, and ask the owner or head mechanic some questions.

Take time to notice what the shop looks like. First impressions are important. A messy garage may mean sloppy work, though there isn't always a correlation. The garage should be clean and well-organized, and the people running it should treat you professionally. Some questions to ask:

What Type of Training Do the Mechanics Have? Ask if mechanics have been certified by the National Institute for Automotive Service Excellence (NIASE), a national training institute that has a voluntary certification program of testing mechanics' competence to perform specific work. A mechanic can be certified in as many as eight categories: engine performance, engine, automatic transmission or transaxle, manual drive-train and axles, suspension, and steering, brakes, electrical systems, and heating and air-conditioning. If mechanics are wearing an ASE patch on their uniforms, it doesn't mean they've been certified in all eight areas. Find out which ones they have been certified in.

Experience also counts. Ask how long the employees have been working as mechanics.

Can You Get a Written Estimate? Most states have laws that require the repair shop to give you a written estimate. Even where it's not required, it's common practice. A responsive mechanic will give you a copy of the estimate before you leave the shop. If you decide to have the shop do the work, the estimate will become your *repair order*— the contract to do the job at the stated price.

The estimate should list the prices of the parts needed and the expected labor charge for installing those parts. Charging more than the estimate without getting your prior approval is illegal in many states. To learn what, if any, amount above the estimate can be charged without your advance approval, call your local Consumer Protection Office.

Will the Garage Return Replaced Parts to You?   Don't be afraid to ask for your old parts back. It's common practice, so don't worry that the mechanic will be offended. The best way to make sure the work is done is to mark your parts *before* they're replaced. You can do this with a regular marker or chalk.

Will the Shop Guarantee Its Parts and Labor?   Shops are not legally obliged to guarantee their work, but some garages do, usually for a specified number of months or miles. It's up to you to find out what's covered.

To benefit from most "parts" warranties, you need to keep good records and to know what's needed to activate the warranty. For instance, if you get a new set of tires but neglect to note your car's mileage at the time they're put on or the installation date on the repair order, the warranty may not be worth the paper it's written on.

Make sure important information—dates, mileage, and type of repair—is fully reflected on the repair order.

Diagnosing the Problem

When you leave your car to be repaired, never make a blanket statement like "Do whatever needs to be done." Don't try to diagnose the car's problems yourself, but make sure the mechanic pays attention to what you say is wrong. This can save time and money.

If problems are too difficult to describe, a good mechanic will suggest using diagnostic equipment or taking the car on a test drive. Both will allow the mechanic to hear, see, or feel problems that you had trouble explaining, and will give the mechanic a place from which to start further diagnosis. However, because this takes time out of the mechanic's schedule, expect an additional charge.

BEFORE AUTHORIZING WORK

It's important to know how shops bill for their time, whether they give estimates on repair work, and whether you're being given the best possible price for the repair.

Understand Billing Practices

Most shops have set fees for labor based on a "book estimate" of how long certain repairs should take. That means if the mechanic does the repair in two hours but the book says it should take four, you'll be charged for four hours. The reverse, of course, is also true.

The "book" that repair shops refer to when making these estimates is actually one of two repair manuals, *Motor's* and *Chilton's.* Both say their estimates are based on "ideal conditions."

Consumer groups have been up in arms for years about flat-rate charges. They argue that the practice is unfair because customers pay more for work than they would if paying by the hour. They also contend flat rates encourage mechanics to rush through repairs, since they are paid based on the number of cars repaired, not the true number of hours worked.

Written Estimates

Most states have laws that require garages to keep your final price to within a specified range of the original estimate, usually 10% to 15%. The only way they can legally charge more than that is with your prior approval. Find out what the law requires in your area by contacting your local Office of Consumer Affairs.

The written estimate is the repair order filled out. Most

mechanics, however, will be too busy to write up a repair order on the spot and will instead want to call you later in the day with specific cost estimates. After you hear what the charges are going to be from the mechanic, your okay over the telephone can be given, or, if convenient, you can drop by to sign the full repair order.

It's important to take a copy of the repair order with you even if it lists only your name, address, phone number, and information about what you think is wrong with the car. If your hunches about what's wrong with the car are right but were not addressed, you'll have written proof that the problem still exists even after the shop worked on the car.

Second Opinions

If you find the estimate too high—because of labor or expensive parts or you just don't trust the mechanic's diagnosis—don't authorize the work, because you may want to get a second or third opinion.

Say the radiator on your 1977 car is leaking. You're told a used radiator, for $95 installed, will eliminate the problem. That's when a second opinion can save you plenty: a can of sealant may also solve the problem, and for about $10. If you don't plan to keep the car much longer, the less expensive route might make the most sense.

If you need a second opinion, think about taking your car into an independent diagnostic center not affiliated in any way with the repair shop you're considering using.

CHECKING REPAIRS

Before paying, you should understand all the charges on the bill you're given. If you don't, ask the mechanic to go over the bill with you.

Make sure you understand exactly what was done and check the bill to make sure the total is less than the allowed increase over the estimate you approved. If you had parts replaced, ask to see them—both the ones removed and the ones installed. In general, ask to see any work that was done on your car whenever possible.

If you've been charged more than you believe is fair, try to have the bill adjusted immediately. This could save you considerable trouble later, and chances are good the mechanic won't want to risk tying up the total payment for a few dollars.

Pay the bill by credit card. If repairs are done incompetently, fraudulently, unnecessarily, or without your permission, you can legally refuse to pay your credit card bill. A second option is to pay by check. You'll be able to stop payment if trouble arises. This puts the garage in the position of having to sue you to collect instead of forcing you to sue the garage for reimbursement.

If you paid by credit card, the Fair Credit Billing Act (FCBA), a federal law, allows you to withhold payment for "defective merchandise and services." Conditions apply: You must prove you tried to settle the problem first; the repair cost must exceed $50; and the repair shop must be within 100 miles of your current residence or within your home state. That means if you receive poor service out of state, you cannot withhold your credit card payment.

Be sure you *write* a letter to the credit card company explaining the problem and what you want refunded. The FCBA can be triggered only with written proof. Remember to send a copy of your letter to the repair shop as well. Finally, until the problem is resolved, the credit card company cannot charge you interest on the amount in dispute.

For more information about your credit rights, write to the Federal Trade Commission, Credit Practices Division, Washington, DC 20580.

Another, but less desirable, option is to pay the entire bill and then file a small claims court action for reimbursement of the amount in dispute. This procedure is covered in the next chapter.

CHAPTER **13**

SOLVING PROBLEMS

You investigate and visit several repair shops, ask all
the right questions, get written estimates, authorize specific
work, review bills, get parts returned, and still drive away
hearing the same noise from under the hood.

If this happens, you have several options, including spe-
cialized auto arbitration if it's a new car, before taking your
case to court. This chapter outlines those options. It should
be read in conjunction with the material in Chapter 4.

As soon as you detect a problem, go straight back to the
shop. When you return to a shop to complain about work
that was done for you, you're known in the auto-repair industry as a "comeback." Most shops treat comebacks well.
They have a vested interest in turning you into a satisfied
customer, not someone who will bad-mouth the company.

If appealing to their good business sense doesn't work,
however, you still have other, more formal options.

CONSUMER AGENCIES

Register a complaint in writing with your local Better Business Bureau or Office of Consumer Affairs. Both agencies
deal with auto-repair complaints all the time. If the Consumer Affairs Office is a branch of your local or county
government, it may already be familiar with the shop in

question. A staff person will contact the owner, investigate the complaint, and attempt to mediate on your behalf. If that doesn't resolve the problem, explore the dispute resolution options in Chapter 4.

If you're a new-car owner with repair problems and your state has a lemon law, you probably can use an auto arbitration program.

AUTO ARBITRATION

Lemon laws, in effect in 45 states and the District of Columbia, require manufacturers to make their cars conform to their warranty within a prescribed time or replace the vehicle entirely. How long manufacturers can take to do these repairs varies from state to state. Typically, they are allowed three or four repair attempts on the same major defect, or a total of 30 days (either business days or calendar days, depending on the state) to service the car within the first 12,000 miles or 12 months.

Lemon laws also encourage manufacturers to establish or participate in arbitration programs to resolve customer complaints when repair attempts fail and the warranty expires.

Most manufacturers comply either by: paying an agency, like the Better Business Bureau or American Arbitration Association, to operate such a program; hire an independent group to do it; or run the program themselves. Several states run car-related arbitration programs out of their Consumer Protection Agencies.

What disputes can be arbitrated, who does it, and whether or not you have to go through arbitration before heading to court depends on your state's lemon law. Each state requires something different. The best way to find out what the requirements are is to ask your state's Consumer Protection Agency or the Better Business Bureau.

The following describes some of the better-known automotive arbitration programs.

AUTO LINE

AUTO LINE is a national program established by the Council of Better Business Bureaus to settle disputes between consumers and certain automobile manufacturers who have agreed to arbitrate complaints when mediation fails. General Motors, American Motors, and a dozen foreign car manufacturers have all contracted with the BBB to offer arbitration to their new-car owners. An agreement to refer disputes to AUTO LINE is usually included in the manufacturer's new-car warranty.

In BBB arbitration, when a complaint is filed, a staff person is assigned to negotiate a solution between you and the manufacturer. This may all happen by telephone or in writing. If negotiation fails and the dispute goes to arbitration, each side is allowed to present its case in person, in writing, or by telephone. Most choose an in-person hearing.

Before the hearing, each side is given background information on five arbitrators and asked to rank them in order of preference. The arbitrator with the highest total rank from both sides is selected to hear the case. If there's a tie, the case is heard by a panel of the top three arbitrators selected.

You may bring expert witnesses (for example, a mechanic who inspected the faulty repair) but must notify the other side in advance if you plan to do so. The arbitrator's decision will be binding only on the manufacturer, unless you also agree to be bound. The BBB reports it settled 64.8% of the 28,100 complaints it handled in 1987.

AUTOCAP

AUTOCAP is an acronym for Automotive Consumer Action Panel. It was established by the National Automobile Dealers Association to resolve disputes informally between new-car and -truck dealers and their customers. As of 1989,

198 dealers participated in these programs and helped finance and run them. AUTOCAP programs are *not* offered in 22 states, and are offered only at the regional level in Florida, New York, Ohio, and Oklahoma.

When you file a dispute with AUTOCAP, it is sent to the dealer, who is given a chance to settle directly with you. If any agreements are made during this time, the dealer is obligated to notify AUTOCAP.

If informal negotiations don't work, AUTOCAP's staff mediates. If that fails, the dispute is submitted in writing to an AUTOCAP panel for review. After a prescribed time, the panel notifies both sides in writing of its decision, but that decision is only advisory; neither side is required to abide by it.

Ford and Chrysler

Both car manufacturers operate their own arbitration programs. In the Ford program, a panel of five (three public members and two dealers) reviews written submissions before issuing a decision. The decision is binding on Ford Motor Company and its dealers, but not on the car buyer.

Chrysler also uses a panel of five: a certified NIASE mechanic, a member of the public, a dealer, a consumer advocate, and a Chrysler representative. The dealer and Chrysler representative are not allowed to vote. Decisions are binding only on the dealer or corporation, not on the buyer unless otherwise agreed to. One catch: Chrysler arbitrates disputes only over its warranty.

Consumer Protection Agencies

Some consumer advocates have voiced skepticism about arbitration programs run by car dealers and manufacturers. Even though the arbitration decisions of these programs are binding only on the car companies, and although panelists with any connection to the auto industry can only offer opinions, statistics show that the decisions still favor car dealers more often than car buyers. The belief is that the panelists who are associated with the industry have a strong influence over the others because they know more about both cars and the arbitration process. This is particularly troubling if consumers are forced to participate in these company-run programs before they can take their case to court.

Eight states—Connecticut, Florida, Massachusetts, Montana, New York, Texas, Vermont, Washington—and the District of Columbia have government panels that hear consumer complaints about cars and car repairs. Three states (California, Delaware, and Ohio) have agencies that regulate the arbitration programs run by manufacturers. If you live in one of these states, all you need to do is file a complaint against the manufacturer with the state's Consumer Protection Agency. It in turn will notify the manufacturer that it is required to participate in arbitration and must report to a hearing within a specified time, typically 15 days.

Court

If direct negotiation and arbitration or private dispute-resolution programs don't work, you can take your case to court. As noted, the automotive industry's arbitration programs are binding only on the car manufacturer or dealer, not you, so taking your claim to them first doesn't change your right to sue—unless, of course, you agree to be bound by the arbitration. If you decide to sue, consider small claims court before municipal or district court (see Chapter 4).

In a civil suit over auto repairs, the burden is on you to prove that the repairs were made in a deceptive or negligent way. If you were quoted an estimate in writing and the final bill exceeds it by much more than the allowed margin, proving deception shouldn't be too hard. However, proving that the mechanic did shoddy work or was negligent may well require testimony by an expert who has inspected the repairs and can testify that the mechanic's work was fraudulent or incompetent. Expect additional time commitments and expenses in lining up such expert testimony, plus the court's fees and, if you decide to be represented, your lawyer's fee.

RESOURCES

For a regional office in your area that offers an automotive arbitration program, contact:

Automotive Consumer Action Program (AUTOCAP)
National Automobile Dealers Association
8400 Westpark Dr.
McLean, VA 22102
(703) 821-7000

BBB AUTO LINE
Council of Better Business Bureaus
1515 Wilson Blvd.
Arlington, VA 22209
(703) 276-0100

Chrysler Customer Arbitration Board
P.O. Box 1718
Detroit, MI 48288
(800) 992-1997

Ford Customer Appeals Board
P.O. Box 1805
Dearborn, MI 48121
(313) 337-6950

Check your local library or bookstore for the following auto-repair guides.

Mr. Badwrench: How You Can Survive the $20 Billion-a-Year Auto-Repair Ripoff. Arthur P. Glickman. Seaview/Wideview Books, 1633 Broadway, New York, NY 10019. 1981 (out of print). 447 pages.

The Armchair Mechanic. Jack Gillis and Tom Kelly. Harper & Row, 10 E. 53rd St., New York, NY 10022. 1988. 176 pages. $8.95.

The Complete Consumer Car Guide. Mike Spaniola. McGraw-Hill Book Co., 1221 Ave. of the Americas, New York, NY 10020. 1987. 249 pages. $9.95.

The Last Chance Garage: A System-by-System Guide to Understanding How Your Car Runs, Why It Occasionally Doesn't, and What You Can Do About It. Brad Sears. Harper & Row, 10 E. 53rd St., New York, NY 10022. 1984 (out of print). 148 pages.

The Shell Auto Care Guide: Tips on Everything You Need to Know as a Car Owner and Driver. Ross R. Olney. Simon and Schuster, 1230 Sixth Ave., New York, NY 10020. 1986 (out of print). 286 pages.

For free brochures that explain how to get hassle-free auto repairs, contact the following:

Communicate with Your Mechanic and Save. Automotive Information Council, P.O. Box 273, Southfield, MI 48037.

Tips on Car Repair. Better Business Bureau, 1515 Wilson Blvd., Arlington, VA 22209.

CHAPTER 14

CONTRACT LANGUAGE

When getting your car repaired, your written estimate and the "repair order" are one and the same. The repair order is so important that many states have laws that excuse you from paying for services if you have not signed one. When you sign it, it authorizes the repair shop to make the repairs or adjustments listed on the order. The following is a typical auto repair contract.

REPAIR ORDER

Customer's Name:—————————————————

Customer's Address:————————————————

Telephone Numbers: *(day)*————— *(night)*—————

Vehicle: *(make)*——— *(year)*—— *(lic. no.)*—————
Odometer:—————————————————————

Customer's description of malfunction: *(explain symptoms)*

—————————————————————————

—————————————————————————

Repair dealer's diagnosis of these malfunctions: *(mechanic's explanation of the problem)*—————————————

—————————————————————————

Promised Completion Date:————————————

Service Required: *(mechanic's description)*—————

—————————————————————————

Parts Description: *(mechanic's list of necessary parts)*———

—————————————————————————

Estimate: Time _____ Parts _____ Labor _____

_____   _____   _____

_____   _____   _____

_____   _____   _____

(Mechanic will enter the hours spent, the prices of parts used, and the labor costs involved.)

Parts total: _____

Labor total: _____

Estimate charge: _____

Storage charge: _____

Total repair charge: _____

Tax: _____

TOTAL ESTIMATE: _____

I hereby authorize and agree to pay for all repairs described in the estimate column: _____

Customer's Signature: _____

Date: _____

I want ___ do not want ___ any replaced parts returned to me.

ORAL AUTHORIZATION OF REPAIRS

Notice to Customer—Estimate:

YOU HAVE THE RIGHT TO RECEIVE A WRITTEN ESTIMATE WHICH IS SIGNED BY YOU AND THE DEALER *BEFORE REPAIR SERVICES ARE AUTHORIZED AND BEGUN.*

If, for technical reasons, we are unable to give you a written estimate at the time we are accepting your vehicle for repair, we would not be permitted to proceed with repairs unless you waive your right to a written estimate.

Therefore, if you wish to waive this right, you may do so by signing the waiver below.

"I hereby waive my right to a written estimate prior to authorizing repairs, but substitute oral communications of the same."

Signed: __*(your signature)*__   Date _____

Notice to Customer:

You will be assessed an estimate charge if you elect not to proceed with repairs after you receive the estimate. If customer orally authorizes repair based on oral communication of the estimate, or modification of estimate costs, reflect oral consent here:

Communication by _____
Authorized by _____
Time _____ Date _____

Service Dealer: Name of Company _____
Date_____

The typical repair order is a preprinted form that comes with three or four carbon copies. The shop gives you a copy, keeps a copy, and sends one to your credit card company if that is the way you are paying.

Make sure the mechanic fills out the repair order completely and accurately to reflect your agreement.

All the following information should be included:

Name and Address: Your full name and current address.

Year, Make, Model, and Tag Number of the car being repaired.

Day and Night Telephone Numbers: It's important to leave a number where you can be reached. The mechanic may need to reach you, for example, to tell you the estimate on repairs or to get your approval before doing additional but necessary work. If a mechanic can't reach you during the day, chances are the car will not be repaired because the mechanic will not want to risk not getting paid for the extra work.

Mileage and Date: Noting the current mileage and date at the time of repair may be important if you later have to rely on the terms of the warranty. You may not receive compensation under the warranty if you have no record of what the mileage was when the parts were installed.

It's also a good idea to keep a record of the dates and mileage at which certain repairs and checkups are done.

That will serve as a "proof of maintenance" record if you ever try to sell your car.

Specific Work to Be Done: Make sure the mechanic identifies in writing on the repair order the "symptoms" of the problem as well as the specific work that will be done. That way, if the symptoms persist (e.g., rattling under the hood) after the repair, you'll have proof the car wasn't repaired properly.

Parts and Labor: Estimates for both parts and labor should be included. They're generally listed in separate columns, side by side. If the mechanic is unable to make estimates when you leave the car, make sure the repair order reflects that no work on the car will begin until you have approved an oral estimate by the mechanic.

Exploratory or Estimate Charges: If part of your car has to be disassembled before an estimate can be given, make sure the mechanic writes down the amount you'll have to pay for that work.

Mechanic's Name: Get the name of the person who will work on your car so you know whom to talk to should you have any questions or should problems occur later.

PART V

LEGAL SERVICES PLANS

CHAPTER **15**

"PREPAID" LAWYERS

Lynne *runs a small boutique in Boston. From time to time, she needs legal advice about handling employees, dealing with customers, and running the store. Her lawyer is always available to help, but at $125 an hour, Lynne is sometimes reluctant to call him.*

Janet recently received a mailing that urged her to join a prepaid legal services plan. For less than $15 a month, it offers her unlimited access to lawyers and certain legal documents for free. While it sounds like a good deal, she wonders if, as a homemaker with three kids, she really needs something like this.

At his new job, Mark receives dental, health, and legal insurance benefits. He expected health insurance, but was surprised to discover that he could also participate in a legal services plan at no cost.

Today, 45 million people participate in legal services plans like those referred to above. Most participate through their unions, associations, or employers. Of those participating, 90% are covered under *group* legal services plans, those usually offered through the workplace and not made available to the public. The remaining 10% belong to *individual* or *private* plans offered directly to the public through direct mail, telemarketing, and door-to-door sales. Ordinarily, anyone can join an individual plan. The exceptions are plans sold solely to the members of a specific credit card company or credit union. Because these individual plans involve payment of an annual or monthly fee *before* legal services can be rendered, they are called *prepaid.*

Prepaid legal plans offer members limited services for a flat yearly or monthly fee. Besides giving ready access to lawyers at lower-than-normal rates for basic legal advice, they eliminate the time clients have to spend "shopping" for a lawyer. Under most plans, lawyers have been preselected for them.

Like health maintenance organizations (HMOs), prepaid legal plans rely on the economy of spreading the risk among a large group of people with the expectation that only a few will take advantage of the benefits. They also mirror HMOs in their emphasis on "preventive law."

In general, legal services plans are beneficial because they allow groups of people to pool their purchasing power to get legal services free or at reduced prices. However, not everyone needs to belong to a plan. Some people go through life without ever needing to contact a lawyer. Others find only an infrequent need for a lawyer's help. Evaluate your legal needs carefully before joining a plan, and then, if you want to join, shop carefully for the plan that best meets those needs. How successful legal services plans will be is still speculative, because they are relatively new.

This chapter explains how the plans operate, the different types available, and their relative advantages and disadvantages. It focuses on plans offered to individuals, but the description of typical benefits should also be helpful to members of group plans.

INDIVIDUAL VERSUS GROUP PLANS

Individual plans usually have a higher per-member operating cost than do group plans because they don't have the economic advantage of drawing on a large pool of available participants.

In group plans, the sponsor (employer, union, or association) may pay all or part of the membership fees. In individual plans, each member is responsible for the entire annual or monthly fee.

A group plan may or may not be *prepaid.* If no advance fee is required of the group or its members, it is "free." The largest "free" group legal plan, called Union Privilege Legal Services, is offered by the AFL-CIO. It is subscribed to by 49 of its labor unions, with over 10 million members.

In an individual, prepaid legal services plan, an annual or monthly fee is paid in advance in exchange for advice from a lawyer and other, specified routine legal help. The fee, normally referred to as the membership or enrollment fee, is paid either by the sponsoring group or by individual members. If the sponsoring group pays the fee, its members are considered *automatically* enrolled. If members pay, membership begins only after the fee is paid.

Whether it's a group or private plan, a *plan administrator* is responsible for promoting the plan, handling its finances, enrolling members, and paying the fees owed to participating lawyers.

GOVERNMENT REGULATION

At least 25 states have specific legislation that governs the way these plans can operate. Some states regulate plans as insurance, while others have statutes that give special jurisdiction to the insurance commissioner but treat the plans as special entities.

To find out how a particular plan is regulated in your state, contact the state insurance commissioner, listed in the telephone book under your state government offices, or the National Resource Center for Consumers of Legal Services, whose address and phone number are on page 153.

WHAT PLANS OFFER

Because members can consult lawyers without charge, they tend to go to them early, to use them as advisers, and to seek their opinions on subjects not normally referred to lawyers. The adage "An ounce of prevention is worth a pound of cure" is applied on the theory that early information can prevent the need for expensive intervention down the line.

The type, size, coverage, and cost of these plans vary widely. The coverage can also change depending on the state you live in. For instance, Prepaid Legal Services, Inc., operates several different plans; the one available in California is different from the one in Oklahoma.

Most plans, group or individual, offer help in selecting a lawyer, unlimited legal counseling, telephone and letter follow-ups, will-drafting, document review, and reduced rates for legal matters that go beyond what's offered for the annual membership fee. Some offer litigation services.

Help in Selecting Lawyers

Under most plans, the administrator decides which lawyer will be assigned to your legal matter. A few plans allow you to select your own lawyer or to select from a panel of lawyers. The advantage of getting a single lawyer or group of lawyers to pick from is that you don't have to spend time "shopping." The disadvantage is that you lose control and freedom to choose whom you'll work with.

We suggest that when you evaluate plans, you ask if you will be allowed to switch lawyers if the one you work with turns out to be unsatisfactory. Find out how difficult this is to do. Is the plan receptive to such requests, or will you be forced to wait a long time because you want a different lawyer?

Ask also if you can get advance information about the

plan's participating lawyers. Typically, such advance information is given only to members who ask for it. Try to find out how long the plan lawyers have been in practice, what areas of law they practice, and whether they carry malpractice insurance. (HALT research shows that plan lawyers have generally been in practice at least five years and are required by plan administrators to carry malpractice insurance.)

Unlimited Telephone Counseling

Most plans offer unlimited telephone consultation. In other words, you can pick up the telephone during normal working hours and get a lawyer at the other end without worrying about the cost. Typically, the number of calls you can make is unlimited, as long as each call is about a new matter. There's also no limit on the amount of time you spend talking. However, you cannot keep calling back about the same problem. Members use this service to get quick advice about such things as resolving a problem with a neighbor, business, or service professional or dealing with traffic violations, simple estate-planning questions, or housing or rental agreements.

With some plans, you do not always get to speak to the same lawyer and therefore have to establish a new relationship, explain who you are and what the problem is, and evaluate again the competence of the person you're speaking to.

If you like the idea of developing a continuing working relationship with one lawyer, ask if that can be accommodated by the plan you're considering.

Office Visits

Under most plans, you also have the option of an in-person visit for any new legal problems. Each office consultation usually has a time limit of one hour or less, however.

If you want to meet with the lawyer more than once on the

same legal matter, you will be charged at the plan's hourly rate. That can be from $50 to $100 an hour. Incurring additional expenses this way can be avoided, however, if you can resolve legal matters over the telephone or by asking the lawyer to make a call or write a letter on your behalf.

Follow-ups

Follow-up correspondence, by either telephone or letter, is included under most plans. Some plans allow their lawyers to handle an unlimited number of calls or free letters on your behalf, but others limit such follow-up work. For example, a lawyer may be able to make only one call *or* write one letter on your behalf per problem, per year of membership. If you think you require a lot of lawyer intervention (for example, to deal with ongoing business or unruly-neighbor problems), you'll want a plan that doesn't restrict the amount of "follow-up" help a lawyer can give you.

Documents

For your membership fee, most plans also draft a simple will and review legal documents like rental agreements, incorporation papers, and repair contracts. A few plans go beyond this, adding documents such as deeds or powers of attorney.

Even simple legal documents like wills can cost as much as $200 in some parts of the country. A legal services plan will draw up a will and provide other benefits for less than that. Be careful, however, when shopping for a plan. Find out what's meant by a "simple will" and whether it will take care of your full estate-planning needs. For example, can a "simple will" include drawing up a minor's trust? How many beneficiaries can be named? Does the plan charge extra if you need to make changes down the line? Some plans include changes *(codicils)* at no extra charge. Will the plan charge extra for your spouse's will?

Does the plan limit the number and length of legal documents you can submit for free review each year? Most plans don't limit the number, but do limit how many pages each document can have—usually fewer than 10 pages. Some plans also refuse to review documents that don't have your name on them. In sum, if drafting documents is a major concern, you would do well to consider an appropriate plan.

Reduced Rates

Plans may also offer guaranteed prices on more complex legal matters, like complex estate planning, real estate transactions, adoptions, and divorces. This can be a savings, but it can also be a money drain in disguise. Check prices with lawyers outside the plan to make sure you're getting the best deal and the most suitable lawyer for your task. You might also consider handling some of your legal matters on your own to keep legal costs down. For example, a plan may offer "name changes for $155," which sounds reasonable, but only until you learn you can easily change your name on your own by going down to the courthouse and filing a piece of paper—for a nominal filing fee.

Litigation Services

Don't expect legal services plans to handle any litigation for free. Most do not provide free lawyer representation in court, and of those that do, most exclude criminal cases, services for which a percentage fee is generally charged (such as personal-injury suits), and appeals. Prepaid Legal Services, Inc., for example, provides lawyer representation for members when they are being sued, but not for members who file lawsuits against someone else.

Most plans do, however, provide free advice about litigation and will appoint a litigation lawyer to represent you at reduced hourly rates. Make sure any appointed lawyer is qualified to handle your case. You may find a more qualified and competitively priced lawyer off the plan.

Other Considerations

Ask where the plan is available and whether you can still get coverage if you move or travel out of state. Will the plan accommodate your needs if you live in Ohio but get into trouble with an auto repair shop or traffic court in Michigan?

By making access easier and less expensive, plans encourage people who have legal questions or problems to consult lawyers more often, but you should be careful of becoming too dependent on lawyers. Instead of meeting the plans' objective of lowering legal expenses, such dependency could end up increasing your legal costs.

TYPES OF PLANS

Legal services plans vary considerably but divide into two basic categories—access and comprehensive plans.

Access Plans

These concentrate on giving members easy access to lawyers for routine legal services. They are typically offered to individuals, and provide free and often unlimited telephone consultations with lawyers, a review of legal documents up to six or seven pages long, and preparation of a simple will. For more complex legal matters, members are referred to a panel of participating lawyers who agree to perform legal services at discounted prices.

Comprehensive Plans

As their name implies, these cover every legal need you have. They are offered only to groups, *not* to individual members of the public. Typically, an employer sponsors a comprehensive plan as a benefit to employees, who participate for free.

Comprehensive plans give the same benefits as access plans and then some. For example, at no additional cost to the employee, lawyers draft any legal document and provide legal representation in or out of court. The plans even reimburse their members for legal expenses or fees they incur (for example, defending against traffic citations).

Open and Closed Panels

All plans also can be distinguished by how they deliver legal services to their members—through one of two arrangements: *closed panels* or *open panels.* Premiums in open-panel systems are generally higher than in closed-panel systems for a simple reason: Open panels give you more choices among lawyers.

Most plans operate closed panels, whereby an agreement is reached with a limited number of lawyers to provide legal assistance to all plan members. In general, for a set price the plan manager either hires a group of lawyers to work for plan members or contracts with a law firm to do all the work. Closed plans generally offer you a greater variety of legal services *and* lower premiums.

One disadvantage of the closed-panel system is that members have little or no voice in choosing which lawyers do their legal work. Some closed plans assign you to a specific lawyer, others allow you to choose one from a limited list. Because legal advice is only as good as the lawyer giving it, it's important to find out if you can dismiss an unsatisfactory lawyer and select or be appointed to another.

Open-panel plans allow you to choose your lawyer from a list. Under this system, each lawyer is paid only for the work performed. The lawyer agrees to a schedule of fixed fees for the services offered. Each lawyer is paid by the plan as the specific work is done, much as doctors are paid by health insurance companies. In open-panel systems, while you have greater freedom of choice, lawyers are not guaranteed a certain amount of legal business from the plan and therefore have little incentive to charge below their normal rates.

SHOPPING FOR A PLAN

1. If you already have a lawyer who is frequently available and charges reasonable prices, there is probably little reason to join a plan.

2. If you have a legal problem that needs immediate attention, spend your time and energy looking for appropriate help, not shopping for a plan. Even though you may find a plan that assigns you to a lawyer immediately, you're leaving it to chance that you'll be referred to the best lawyer for the problem at hand. It makes more sense to shop for a legal services plan when you have time and aren't influenced by specific, pressing concerns.

3. Send for information on all available plans. The National Resource Center for Consumers of Legal Services can send you a list of the major ones and their addresses. Simply send a stamped, self-addressed envelope to the address on page 153.

4. Don't be pressured by aggressive sales language in direct mail solicitation into signing anything before you're ready. These plans need many members to successfully continue offering low membership rates. Your money will be accepted when you're ready to give it.

5. Learn all you can about the history and operations of the organization that's running the program to be sure it's reputable. Plan representatives should be willing to answer such questions as:

- How long has the program been in operation? (New plans have yet to demonstrate a track record or develop a full array of smoothly operating services.)
- How many lawyers participate in the plan? Has the number increased or decreased during the past year? (A growing plan is healthier and more likely to meet your future needs.)
- Are panels open or closed?
- Can you switch lawyers if you're unhappy with the one appointed to you?
- How big is the plan? How many people have enrolled?
- Does it include a grievance or complaint system?
- Does it allow you to evaluate services annually and drop your membership if you're unsatisfied?
- What happens if the plan goes out of business? Do you get a refund?
- What references can they furnish?

CHAPTER 16

SOLVING PROBLEMS

If you have a problem with a legal services plan lawyer, your options are the same as when you have a problem with any lawyer, plus one: You can also turn to plan administrators for help.

Unfortunately, many of the usual places you can turn to for help with consumer problems, such as government-run Consumer Affairs Offices and private Better Business Bureaus, do not handle complaints against lawyers.*

As soon as you become aware of a potential lawyer-client problem, contact your lawyer to discuss it and make sure it's not simply a breakdown in communication. Sometimes problems can be resolved quickly with a telephone call and follow-up letter. Communicate concerns in writing to develop a written record of your attempts to resolve problems.

If your plan lawyer refuses to communicate with you or refuses to try to resolve the problem responsibly, complain to the plan sponsor. If an "800" hot line is available, call there. Ask a company representative to serve as an intermediary between you and the lawyer. The company can't compel the lawyer to act a certain way or to refund your money, but it does have the power to remove the lawyer from its list

---

*A full discussion of handling problems with your lawyer can be found in HALT's *Using a Lawyer* by Kay Ostberg, Random House, 1990. Most of the information in the remainder of this chapter is derived from that book and is presented here only as a brief overview.

of approved attorneys. While that may not help you directly, the threat of being booted may be incentive enough for a lawyer to shape up. Whether or not the lawyer is removed, if you chose wisely, your plan probably will let you pick a new lawyer to continue your case.

If direct negotiation with the lawyer and working through the plan administrator don't solve your problem, you have four options:

Client Security Trust Funds

In every state except Maine and New Mexico, the state bar association has a special fund to reimburse money stolen from clients by their lawyers. Whether or not you can collect from the fund is up to the bar association, however. You have no legal *right* to collect from the fund or to challenge it if your claim is rejected. Also, most programs limit the amount they will refund (usually $15,000 to $25,000), regardless of how much was stolen. To find out how to file a claim with your state program and what its limitations are, contact the state bar association.

Fee Arbitration

If you have a dispute over your lawyer's fee, you may be able to take it to a fee-arbitration program, also run by the bar. Unfortunately, arbitration is not always available, and in most states lawyers unwilling to arbitrate can't be required to. In any case, these programs are of limited value because most of the arbitrators are lawyers and because they aren't allowed to consider malpractice issues in deciding whether or not to reduce a lawyer's fee. To find out more about fee arbitration, contact your state bar.

Attorney Discipline

Every state has a lawyer-discipline agency, many of them run by the state bar. You can ask your state's discipline committee to reprimand, suspend from practice, or disbar your lawyer. You can't receive compensation through this process, however, even if misconduct is proven.

Lawyer-discipline systems are slow, secret, and lenient. Of the approximately 70,000 complaints filed each year, fewer than 2% result in suspension or disbarment. Nevertheless, people should file complaints because this is the only forum that has authority to remove unethical or incompetent lawyers from practice. Each complaint helps establish the pattern necessary to convince an agency to take action.

Suing for Malpractice

As always, suing should be your final recourse because of the time and expense involved. If you do win a malpractice suit, you can be awarded money and, sometimes, attorney fees. However, legal malpractice cases are extremely difficult and expensive: You must prove that your lawyer did not use the skill, care, and diligence ordinarily used by lawyers *and* that, as a result of this negligence, you lost money. To prove your lawyer failed to use appropriate care, you must hire an expert witness willing to testify to that. To prove the lawyer's misconduct caused you to lose money, in some instances you must retry the original case you thought the lawyer should have won. This is called the "trial within a trial," and can make your case very expensive indeed.

Finally, it can often be hard to find a lawyer willing to represent you in suing another lawyer for malpractice. Lawyers estimate that if your claim is not worth more than $10,000, it is not economical to sue. Many lawyers won't even take cases unless the potential "win" is at least $50,000. Don't go it alone, however. Taking on your adversary on your adversary's turf, the courtroom, is not easy. If you are considering a malpractice suit, consult HALT's *Directory of Lawyers Who Sue Lawyers,* which contains a state-by-state list of lawyers willing to sue for legal malpractice, plus tips on how to assess the merits of your malpractice case.

RESOURCE

For more information on legal services plans, contact:

The National Resource Center for Consumers of Legal
 Services
1444 Eye St. NW, 8th Floor
Washington, DC 20005
(202) 842-3503

CHAPTER 17

CONTRACT LANGUAGE

The "contract" to join an individual legal services plan is a simple form that briefly describes the agreement and refers you to a brochure for more details about the terms and benefits of membership. The form simply requires your signature and, if you're paying by credit card, the number.

The information you need to know about the plan is covered *not* in the agreement form but in the brochure. Most such brochures are written in plain language with a lot of sales talk. These promotional brochures list both the free benefits you get by joining the plan and the benefits that are available at reduced rates.

The following section describes one typical plan, Montgomery Ward Enterprises Legal Services Plan, mailed to Montgomery Ward credit card holders. An identical plan, Legal Services Plan of America, also marketed by Montgomery Ward, is offered by major credit card companies and banks to their subscribers.

This plan is representative of an "access" legal services plan. Clarification of the benefits is based both on this contract and on the company's related materials. One final note: if at any time you want to drop your subscription, all you need to do is write a letter to that effect to the plan's administrator.

MONTGOMERY WARD ENTERPRISES IS PROUD TO OFFER . . .

A new, much needed approach to legal services protection which can immediately benefit you and your family.

Join this plan and you and your immediate family will be covered for much of the personal and family legal work you would normally expect to require.

For a monthly fee of only $6.75, you and your family will immediately retain the professional services of a firm of attorneys located near your home or office. The plan attorneys are qualified, in private practice and are licensed by your state.

2,380 lawyers from 680 law firms participate in this plan. To be eligible, they must have been in practice at least three years. According to a plan representative, its lawyers have practiced an average of 13.5 years. However, keep in mind that whether they're qualified to handle your case has more to do with their experience at handling similar problems than the fact they're licensed. All practicing lawyers have to be licensed by the state.

This language also states that you and your immediate family are covered. "Immediate family" includes your spouse and dependents.

Coverage commences the moment you are enrolled in the Montgomery Ward Enterprises Legal Services Plan.

IMPORTANT: This enrollment period is limited. Your Enrollment Certificate *must* be received on or before the deadline indicated in order to be eligible. No exceptions will be permitted.

This is an example of a high-pressure sales pitch. *Ignore it.* If you don't respond "in time," you will probably receive another solicitation later, with a different deadline, or you can call or send in your membership information at any time.

The Comprehensive Montgomery Ward Enterprises Legal Services Plan provides much of the legal services normally required.

As a member of the Montgomery Ward Enterprises Legal Services Plan, you will be banding together with thousands of others who will enjoy the benefits of comprehensive legal services.

In effect, joining the Montgomery Ward Enterprises Legal Services Plan puts a group of experienced, professional attorneys on retainer for you and your family. All you pay is the modest monthly fee of just $6.75.

The Plan has two parts:
A) Prepaid Benefits *(services covered by your membership fee)*
B) Bonus Benefits *(services not covered but offered at reduced prices)*

The information on the following pages details your benefits and addresses a number of important questions you may have.

Please read this material *now.* Remember, this enrollment period is limited. Your Enrollment Certificate *must* be returned on or before the deadline indicated in order to be eligible. No exceptions will be permitted.

Exceptions are the rule here. If they weren't, the plan would go out of business in short order. This sales letter from Montgomery Ward appears with a number of different "deadlines," depending when it was mailed. These aren't true deadlines; they are simply "Buy now!" exhortations.

PREPAID BENEFITS

1) *Unlimited Consultation and Advice by Phone or Mail*
As soon as we enroll you in the Montgomery Ward Enterprises Legal Services Plan, your plan attorneys will immediately be at your service for consultation and advice during normal business hours concerning any personal or family legal problem you might have. You'll never again have to hesitate about seeking advice from your plan attorneys be-

cause you're concerned about cost. Simply call the plan attorneys at the phone number on your membership card and they will be ready to help you.

This states that you can call and get a lawyer as soon as the company processes your check or gets your credit card number and sends you a membership card. On that card is the telephone number of the law firm that has been preselected for you. The plan administrator will pick a lawyer from the firm that's nearest you. Each time you call or write, you will get that same law firm. (Other plans use a lawyer "hot line" to take calls. Their members do not speak to the same lawyer twice, except by chance.)

The Montgomery Ward plan also includes an "800" number to call if you want an administrator to assign you a different lawyer. Under this plan, you are not given information on a variety of lawyers and then allowed to pick the one you want, but you may later ask to switch if you're not happy with the lawyer picked for you.

Your lawyer is responsible for answering all your personal or family legal problems. While most plans provide such free consultation on any legal matter, including criminal matters or litigation problems, you will have to pay extra if you need in-court representation. The lawyers in most plans accept such additional legal work at reduced hourly rates.

The number of times you can call or write your lawyer is unlimited in this plan, as is how long your telephone call can last. However, you must call during "normal" business hours. Ask what's normal for *your* lawyer. It may be 9:00 A.M. to 5:00 P.M., or 7:00 A.M. to 3:00 P.M. Under this plan, anyone in your immediate family can call, even your fifteen-year-old.

2) *Unlimited Legal Letters and Phone Calls on Your Behalf*
It could be quite costly, without the Montgomery Ward Enterprises Legal Services Plan, to have an attorney handle legal

matters because you would normally be charged hourly rates for your attorney's time. Under the plan, your plan attorneys will make telephone calls and write letters which you both agree are necessary, at no additional charge to you.

Under this plan, your appointed lawyer will handle all the telephone calls and letters you need to resolve your legal problem. The number of such letters and phone calls that can be made for you is unlimited in most states.

To comply with state regulations, however, Arkansas, Indiana, Nebraska, and Virginia residents must pay $5 for each letter or phone call a plan lawyer handles for them, and New York residents are limited to three letters or phone calls a year, no more than two of which can be related to the same matter. Other plans, such as Prepaid Legal Services, allow only one letter or call per problem per year.

The Montgomery Ward plan also requires that your lawyer agree that the letters and calls you want are really necessary to resolve your problem. If you disagree, the plan administrator may be able to help you and the attorney resolve the disagreement. If not, see Chapter 16, Solving Problems.

It isn't as bad as it may seem, however, because the lawyer has an incentive to keep you satisfied. Because the lawyer can be required to handle an unlimited number of calls and letters for you, it's in the lawyer's interest to resolve the problem as quickly as possible. Also, the lawyer hopes you will develop a good working relationship so you will return for more help on matters that aren't covered by the plan.

3) *A Simple Personal Will for You and Your Immediate Family*
As soon as you receive your membership card for the plan, you can request the preparation of a simple will for you or any member of your immediate family. Don't worry about cost, you're totally covered. What's more, if at any time it is necessary to have your will updated, your plan attorneys will attend to it at no additional charge. This is just one example of the

many benefits you receive as a member of the Montgomery Ward Enterprises Legal Services Plan.

This is typical of most plans. It says you and anyone in your immediate family can get a simple will executed. (In New York, members and spouses are each entitled to one free will and annual updates. Arkansas, Nebraska, and Virginia residents are charged $15 for this service.)

As defined by the plan, a simple will "distributes the property generally and does not involve any trusts, complex tax considerations or guardianships for minor children." It's important to find out in advance how "simple" a will must be to qualify. Be sure the will you get takes care of your needs. If you want more complex estate planning (e.g., creating a trust for your children or leaving the dining-room set to your daughter and the Oriental rugs to your son), the "simple will" is not for you. It is only for people who want to leave their property to one person or divide it equally among a number of people. If you need something more complex, you can get it, but at additional cost.

4) *Document Review*

Many legal problems are the result of parties entering into undesirable or unfair agreements. You may avoid a potential costly legal dispute by having an attorney examine an agreement before you sign it. Yet, all too often, many citizens fail to do so (and suffer as a consequence) because they are fearful of the expense. You need not fret about such costs. Your plan attorneys will review any legal document as long as six pages—leases, real estate papers, installment and rental contracts, promissory notes, bills of sale, powers of attorney, affidavits, and a variety of other legal documents. Cost? You're covered! (If the document is longer than six pages, it will be reviewed at the guaranteed rate of no more than $50 an hour.)

This plan allows for an unlimited number of legal documents to be reviewed by your plan lawyer during your membership, as long as each document is no longer than six pages. Most plans offer a document review option and place similar restrictions on it.

Under this plan, you do not need to be named in the document to have it reviewed. For example, you could present a rental agreement for review before signing it. Some plans do require your name to be on any document you ask to have reviewed.

5) *Warranty Problems*

Your plan attorneys will assist you on your warranty problems. They'll write letters and make phone calls on your behalf. And if you have to go to court on the matter, they can be there to represent you for no more than $50 an hour.

Both service and product warranties are covered by this plan. For example, you are promised free advice or help if you're having a problem with the way a contractor renovated your kitchen or the way a vacuum cleaner operates before its warranty expires.

6) *Initial Face-to-Face Consultation on Any New Legal Problem*

When you are confronted by a new legal problem that can't be handled by telephone or letters, you may consult with your plan attorneys on a face-to-face basis. You are completely covered on a prepaid basis for any and all such initial personal consultations.

This entitles you to one visit to your lawyer's office for each new problem. If you must discuss the same legal problem in person more than once, it will cost you $50 an hour. That rate is a good price in most areas of the country and a great price in larger metropolitan areas. However, your plan lawyer will discuss the matter over the telephone as often as you want, within reason, at no extra charge.

Some plans allow unlimited office visits, while others don't allow even one.

7) *Advice on Small Claims Court*

If you go to small claims court to settle a grievance, your plan attorneys will give you advice on how to prepare and present your case and how to complete necessary forms.

This is true of all plans. The type of help you get on any legal matter depends on the lawyer giving it, however. Some lawyers get a lot of requests for information about small claims court and have prepared written materials on the process for their clients. Others give clients a brief "walk-through," and still others offer to help fill out the necessary court papers and discuss presentation styles.

Your lawyer will not go to court with you unless, again, you are willing to pay extra. At $50 an hour, travel, waiting, and court time can add up. Get whatever information you can in advance and then handle this kind of claim on your own. In any event, many small claims courts will not allow you to have a lawyer in court with you.

8) *Advice on Government Programs*

Your plan attorneys will assist you in locating the appropriate government agency to handle your Social Security, Medicare, veteran's benefits or other matters. Then they'll advise you on how the agency operates, where to go and what benefits you may be entitled to receive.

Some lawyers will put you in touch with the right people and give you information that can make collecting benefits a lot less trying. Others may be less acquainted with procedures. Expect the lawyer to charge extra if you ask to have the benefits collected for you.

9) *$1,000 Emergency Bail Bond Service*

Should you or any member of your immediate family ever need bail in a hurry, you need only call the 24-hour toll-free Bail Bond Hot Line phone number and a bail bond of up to $1,000 will be posted as soon as possible.

Depending on the state you live in, a $1,000 bail bond may cover only misdemeanors, traffic offenses, and some minor felonies. For example, many judges set bond at $1,000 in shoplifting and speeding cases. For more serious offenses, some judges demand $10,000 bail. Bond companies collect a 10 percent cash deposit for posting your bond.

Before taking advantage of this provision, ask how long you have to reimburse the bond and whether you'll be charged interest. Under this plan, you are not charged interest and you have at least thirty days to repay. Bail bond services are not included under the plans offered by either Hyatt or Prepaid Services.

BONUS BENEFITS

In addition to your prepaid benefits, the Montgomery Ward Enterprises Legal Services Plan gives you bonus benefits—which provide you with guaranteed maximum fees for six major legal matters, guaranteed rates on contingent fee matters and guaranteed maximum rates on all matters.

GUARANTEED MAXIMUM FEES
FOR SIX LEGAL MATTERS

Service	Maximum Fees for Plan Members
Uncontested Adoption*	$185.00*
Name Change	$155.00
Non-Commercial Real Estate Closing	$175.00
Will with Minor's Trust	$170.00
Non-Support of Spouse or Children	$240.00
Uncontested Divorce**	$210.00**

*Does not include termination of parental rights.
**Subject to a limit of net marital assets of $70,000, no children under the age of 18, the defendant spouse is not represented by an attorney and all issues are agreed to without negotiation by the plan attorney.

While the prices for these "simple" legal matters are relatively low compared to those of private lawyers in most places, be aware that many of these matters can be taken care of *without a lawyer* for even less.

Two quick examples are name changes and uncontested adoptions. To legally change your name in most states, all you need do is file a "name change" form with the appropriate court, then personally notify people and businesses you think should know about your new name. The cost of filing is usually $100 or less. Many uncontested adoptions also never involve a lawyer. Instead, an adoption agency tells the adopting parents what they need to know, including how to prepare for a hearing.

Still, if you don't feel comfortable handling legal matters on your own, these prices are at least better than average. According to a 1988 study by the National Resource Center for Consumers of Legal Services, the national average for real estate closings is $436, for uncontested divorces is $506, and for simple wills is $83.

MAXIMUM RATES FOR CONTINGENCY FEE CASES

This is an important benefit. Contingency fee cases occur when you are suing someone for damages such as in personal injury and collection cases. The attorney agrees to being paid a contingency fee, a percentage of any financial recovery, rather than an hourly rate. It is important that you have control of this fee, as it directly impacts the net amount of any settlement or award you may actually receive.

Attorney contingency fees can go as high as 45%. (In some cases, the fees have been even higher!) You won't have any such worries. Your plan attorney's percentage is *guaranteed* not to exceed 29% of the recovery if settled before trial, 36% if settled or recovered during or after trial, or 40% if settled or awarded after an appellate brief is prepared. And it may, in fact, be even lower. In matters in which state statutes set the contingent attorney fee, the attorney fee charged will be 10% less than the statutory rate or the attorney's usual fee, whichever is less. For example, in Michigan, personal injury contingency fee rates are limited to 33.3%. There, if an attorney typically charges 33.3%, you would receive the plan rate of 29.9%—a 10% reduction.

This is *not* much of a discount. Contingency fees, almost always used in personal-injury cases, normally run about 30%, not 45%. If you hire a lawyer under this type of arrangement, shop around and see if you can get one to agree to a lower percentage. You may be able to bargain an outside lawyer down from 29%, since you already know you're guaranteed that rate by the plan's offer of 10% off the lawyer's usual rate.

Under standard contingency fee arrangements, if you win, the lawyer gets a percentage of the "take"; if you lose, the lawyer gets expenses but nothing else. The theory is that the lawyer should collect a large slice of the winnings in exchange for the risk of getting nothing; but be assured that any lawyer interested in taking your case is fairly confident of winning. In fact, the more lawyers you find interested in your case, the better your chances of bargaining down the percentage fee.

GUARANTEED RATES ON HOURLY CHARGES!

On any matter not covered elsewhere, you will pay no more than $50 per hour. For instance, after your initial prepaid personal consultation, your plan attorneys will provide you with further personal consultation or represent you in court for no more than $50 per hour on matters where no maximum fee is involved.

This low hourly rate is much lower than many attorneys would charge the general public. Attorneys' hourly rates vary by years of experience, geographic location and other factors. However, one recently published survey reports the median rate that attorneys charge nationally for family law and general personal matters is $75 an hour—yet you pay no more than $50 an hour when you use Plan Attorneys.

Plus, remember that your initial personal consultation with your plan attorneys concerning any of these legal problems is already part of your prepaid benefits.

According to the 1988 study by the National Resource Center for Consumers of Legal Services, the average hourly rate for lawyers is between $85 and $90. That makes the $50 hourly rate charged by this plan pretty good, especially when you consider that lawyers in large metropolitan areas charge as high as $150 or $200 an hour. Again, however, before hiring a plan lawyer, explore other options for getting routine legal work done, and shop for a lawyer who has the experience to handle the matter at hand. For instance, a legal clinic may be able to help for less money or you may be able to do the work on your own with a do-it-yourself publication.

PART VI

RENTING
A HOME

CHAPTER 18

RENTALS

Mary and Nancy have lived in their apartment three years and don't plan to move. Their landlord tells them he needs the apartment for his mother, who is being discharged from a nursing home in two weeks, and they will have to move.

Tim has rented his apartment five years and has kept it clean. He gives the landlord the required notice and moves out, but weeks later, he receives a check for only half of his original security deposit. The landlord says he kept the remainder to paint the apartment.

Jim rents from Jennifer, who lives downstairs. To save money, Jennifer stopped using an exterminator service, and Jim's apartment has become infested with mice. After unsuccessful attempts to get satisfaction from Jennifer, he calls the local housing authority to report the housing code violation and refuses to pay further rent until the mice are exterminated. A week later, Jennifer notifies Jim that he has to move.

In all these cases, the renters have rights they may not be aware of. This chapter explains such rights and what role the rental agreement plays in defining them.

For many, the first major contract we sign is when we rent a first house or apartment. Though most of us don't read our leases carefully beyond checking the amount of monthly rent and the length of the lease, it is only by understanding our rights and obligations that we can feel safe and comfortable in our home.

In recent decades, contract laws and court decisions have significantly changed the rights and responsibilities of landlords and tenants. As a result, the lease has evolved into what is basically a consumer contract, under which the landlord is obliged to maintain the property in a safe, sanitary, and habitable condition.

Pro-tenant laws have proliferated in most large urban areas, where the large number of renters constitutes a natural lobbying group. Some tenants' groups are so well organized they operate telephone "hot lines" that offer free advice. In small towns, however, landlord-tenant laws are less likely to be as pro-tenant, and consumer information is less likely to be generally available.

TYPES OF AGREEMENTS

Every rental arrangement is governed by a contract. You will have either an oral agreement or a written agreement, called a *lease.*

Oral Agreements
Without putting it in writing, you and the landlord may verbally agree on the unit to be occupied, the date you will move in, the amount of rent you'll pay, and how often you'll pay it. Although such an oral lease is legal if the term is less than the limit specified in your state's laws (usually one year), *don't* rely on it unless you insist on flexibility and all the risk that entails.

An oral lease will allow you to move out on fairly short notice (typically a month), but you'll have no written record of any promises the landlord made—for instance, to make repairs or to allow you to move in by a specific date. Also, an unwritten lease allows the landlord some flexibility, too: for instance, to be rid of you or to raise the rent on fairly short notice. It's best to avoid oral rental agreements.

Leases

Leases are written rental agreements that cover a fixed time, typically a year. However, they can cover an indefinite or shorter time. The terms, such as the rent you pay, can't be changed while the lease is in effect. This means that a lease offers less flexibility but more security than an oral rental agreement, for both the tenant and the landlord.

BASIC RENTAL CONCEPTS

(This section should be read in conjunction with the explanations of standard lease terms in Chapter 20 and with the next chapter, Solving Problems.)

Housing Discrimination

Federal law forbids landlords to refuse to rent to anyone because of race, color, religion, national origin, or sex. The laws of most states and of some local governments prohibit discrimination on other grounds, such as marital status, sexual orientation, age, physical disability, political affiliation, or the presence of children.

Landlords may not refuse to rent on those grounds, nor may they discriminate in other ways, such as raising the rent for such people. Some landlords are exempt from these laws, however. For example, federal laws don't apply to buildings in which the landlord resides that have fewer than five units.

Landlords also can have valid reasons for refusing to rent. For instance, they may refuse a prospective renter because of a history of nonpayment of rent, or refuse to overcrowd a two-bedroom apartment with a family of seven. It sometimes can be difficult to tell whether a landlord is properly refusing to rent or shielding illegal discrimination behind a valid reason for refusal.

Evictions

All states have laws that govern when a tenant can be asked to leave the rental property, the reasons a landlord can evict, and the notices the landlord has to give before eviction. Typical reasons for allowing evictions include the tenant failing to pay rent or violating the lease by using the residence to operate a business or by housing too many people. Even when such a violation is invoked, however, landlords must follow strict guidelines set out in statutes and court decisions.

In most states, landlords must give notice at least 30 days before an eviction hearing is held. In just about every state, the landlord has to prove in court that the tenant received written notice of the hearing within the prescribed time limits.

If your landlord asks the court to evict you for nonpayment of rent, the court may allow you to "cure" this breach by paying the amount you owe. It is always worth attending the eviction hearing because the court may try to help you reach a compromise short of eviction. If the court does order your eviction, you usually are given a short time before you must leave. If you aren't out by that deadline, a state official will physically remove your belongings from the residence and lock you out. Sometimes a landlord can require you to move out even if you have not violated the lease. Many states, for instance, allow a landlord to ask a tenant to leave if extensive renovations are planned, or if the landlord or a family member plans to use the property as a principal residence. Thus, in the example at the beginning of this chapter, Mary and Nancy's landlord can legally ask them to leave so his mother can move into the apartment. The landlord must still give advance notice, however.

Utilities

Some landlords attempt to force tenants to move out by shutting off utilities. This is illegal. If complaining about it doesn't resolve the problem, you can get a court to order the utilities turned back on. In some states, the landlord can be fined under criminal laws, and in every state the tenant has the right to sue for damages. Also, any tenant forced to move out because the landlord shuts off the utilities does not owe rent for the remaining term of the lease.

Housing Codes

Housing codes set minimum standards of health and safety in rental housing in many states, and virtually every city has such a code, because without it, the city would not be eligible for federal urban renewal funds. If conditions in your rental unit do not seem to satisfy code requirements, try to get your landlord to agree in writing to fix them by a specific date. (See page 180 for information on code requirements in your area and how to enforce them.)

An *implied warranty of habitability* applies to rental agreements in many places. This means that, whether or not it is written into the lease, the landlord must keep rental property habitable. Some local housing codes define habitability; in other places, habitability standards are set out in state law, and in still others, court cases have defined habitability. Call your local housing agency and ask about code requirements in your area.

Before moving into a rental home, walk through it with the landlord and list all minor problems you can find (such as small cracks) so both you and the landlord know what you will and will not be responsible for when you move out. Some landlords will already have a list of items for you to check; add to that list if it is not complete.

In our opening example of Jim, Jennifer, and the mice, in most states Jim would be well within his rights to withhold rent, and Jennifer would have illegally retaliated by attempting to evict him. (Allowing mice to proliferate violates most, if not all, housing codes.) In some states, tenants may legally withhold their rent until housing code violations are corrected. After the violations are corrected, the tenant must pay the rent, but the amount owed may be reduced by a housing or landlord-tenant court, depending on the nature or seriousness of the violation. It is usually illegal to retaliate against a tenant for reporting a housing code violation.

Rent Control

Many localities have rent control laws, especially cities where affordable housing is scarce; these laws vary greatly. The "controls" on how much your rent can be increased may allow the landlord a specified percentage return on the value of the property, restrict annual increases to a specific percentage, or even restrict increases based on each tenant's ability to pay.

Also, rent control laws don't usually apply to all rental units in an area. For instance, they may apply only to landlords who own four or more rental units. Some laws exempt luxury rental housing, while others exempt owner-occupied buildings, new buildings, or single-family dwellings.

Deposits

Landlords may impose special advance fees or deposits as a condition of renting.

A security deposit is the most common. This is money the landlord holds as security against property damage, unpaid rent, and sometimes cleaning costs. Almost all states have laws that govern some aspect of the security deposit: the maximum that can be charged (usually two months' rent), conditions for returning it, the time within which it must be returned, and interest that must be paid on it for the period the landlord held it. Some local laws add other requirements.

In the example at the beginning of this chapter, Tim's

landlord illegally withheld part of the security deposit. Security deposits cannot be used to pay for repairing normal wear and tear on the rental unit, such as repainting after five years. They can be used to cover unpaid rent, however, so if you break your lease by moving out early, rest assured your landlord will use your deposit to cover at least part of any rent lost because of your move. (See Renewing Your Lease, below.)

In some places, landlords charge special cleaning deposits to ensure that the premises are left as clean as they were when the tenant moved in. However, cleaning fees—nonrefundable charges used for cleaning and minor repairs—are not legal in some states. If your landlord attempts to charge such a nonrefundable fee, ask your local rental authority or housing agency if it's legal.

Some landlords require that you pay the *last* month's rent before you move in so that there is no difficulty collecting it when you move out. Be sure you and the landlord spell out, in writing, what these various advance costs are, and whether they are returnable. If you have any doubts, check state and local housing agencies to be sure the landlord is complying with them.

Subleasing and Assigning

Prohibitions on *subleasing* are usually legal. When subleasing is allowed, it's usually subject to the landlord's written approval of the subtenant. Ideally, such a provision in your original lease should state that the landlord can't *unreasonably* withhold approval. Some states' courts read this into leases even when it's not explicitly stated. Although subleasing can be convenient for tenants who, say, leave town for a few months, the tenant remains ultimately responsible to the landlord for the rent, the condition of the property, and the like.

Assigning the lease is not the same as subleasing. It means that someone else replaces you as the tenant in the original lease and you can *both* be held responsible for fulfilling the lease obligations. A lease that allows you to assign usually requires the landlord's consent. If you are the one to whom the lease is being assigned, be sure to get the assignment in writing.

Liability for Damage

The landlord's lease may include language disclaiming responsibility for any property damage or personal injury that results from the landlord's negligence in maintaining the property. In many areas, such a provision is illegal. Again, check with your housing agency.

Waivers

The landlord may include language that waives your right to notice, or the right to a jury trial in disputes over the lease. Most such waivers are illegal. If the landlord tries to take advantage of such a waiver, a court will refuse to enforce it and will void the clause though the rest of the lease will remain valid.

Right to Privacy

Not all states' laws specify when the landlord has a right to enter the rental property, but if a lease says the landlord may enter at any time and for any reason, you may have waived your right to privacy. More typically, leases specify the conditions and times landlords may enter. For instance, in some states landlords must give 24 hours' notice before entering to make repairs and may come in only between 9:00 A.M. and 5:00 P.M. Check with your housing agency for laws regarding your landlord's right to enter. If they don't provide guidelines, make sure it's covered in your lease.

Late Charges

Landlords may charge a *reasonable* fee for late rent payments. In some areas, this amount is limited by law. A *fixed* late charge might range from $5 to $35, depending on the amount of rent, and can be even higher for luxury apartments. An *incremental* late charge might start at $5 for the first day after the grace period and increase $2 every day after that, to a maximum of $25 or $35.

An unreasonable late charge is one that's out of proportion to the rent—for example, $50 for a $250 apartment. If your lease doesn't give you a grace period before the late charge applies—typically, three to five days—it's reasonable to ask for one, but recognize that the landlord may not be required by law to offer it.

Renewing Your Lease

Most leases renew themselves automatically. If yours is silent on the length of the renewal, it will renew itself for the length of the original term (typically, a year). However, the landlord does have the right to raise the rent at each lease's expiration.

If your lease explicitly requires that you return the property to the landlord when the lease expires, except in a few pro-tenant jurisdictions, you will have no right to renewal and will have to negotiate a new lease.

If your lease says nothing about renewal, state laws apply. Some states require you to return the property at the end of the lease term, other states have laws that automatically renew the lease month-to-month. If you want to move at the end of the lease and your lease has an automatic-renewal provision, you must notify the landlord a specified number of days in advance, typically 30. If you give notice, then change your mind and don't leave by the time you promised, you may be charged double rent as a penalty while you *hold over.*

If you decide to move before the lease expires, you may have to pay rent for the remaining life of the lease. If you have an oral agreement or are renting month-to-month, you're only obligated to give the landlord appropriate written notice (usually 30 days), and you aren't responsible for rent beyond that period. If you have a longer-term lease, the landlord must try to rent the property to someone else for the remaining lease period. This is the landlord's obligation to *mitigate damages,* explained in Chapter 2.

It's in your best interest to give written notice as far in advance of your intended moving date as you can, to give the landlord as much time as possible to rent the property to someone else, sparing you at least part of the rent due for the period after you leave. If the property is rented again, you will still have to pay any lost rent, however—either for the time the property was vacant or for any difference between the amount you were paying and any lesser amount the new tenant pays. If you leave before the end of your lease, the landlord will keep your security deposit to cover what you owe.

CHAPTER 19

SOLVING PROBLEMS

Landlord-tenant relations are heavily regulated—by federal, state, county, and city governments. If you have a landlord-tenant problem or anticipate having one, both public and private groups can help advise you on your rights.

Try to settle your dispute through direct negotiation with your landlord, then take your complaint to a rental-housing agency operated by state, county, or city government. They hold hearings on complaints that allege violations of rent-control laws, housing codes, the implied warranty of habitability, and sometimes discrimination. Hearing examiners usually can decide cases and award damages. (Some laws call for triple damages on proven overcharges.) Appeals usually go to a higher administrative body, and from there to court. Complainants may be required to exhaust these administrative remedies before going to court.

If you believe you have been discriminated against in a housing matter, contact your regional office of the Department of Housing and Urban Development (HUD). Addresses are listed in Appendix IV. For information on state or local housing discrimination laws, check with state fair housing offices and civil rights commissions. Both HUD and most state agencies have administrative procedures for filing discrimination complaints and enforcing the laws when violations are found.

Another way to fight discrimination is to sue your landlord

in court, but this makes sense only when you have clear evidence of discrimination and can prove your damages were high. Otherwise, it may not be worth the legal fees and other expenses.

If you believe a rent increase violated rent control laws, find out if your local government has a rent control board. This office can tell you if the laws apply to your landlord and your rental unit, and if they are being applied correctly. Areas with rent control almost always have an administrative procedure for resolving disputes about rent adjustments.

If all or part of your security deposit is withheld unfairly, ask the landlord for a written statement explaining why. If that doesn't work, call your local rental housing agency to learn the procedure for filing a complaint. In some localities, the agency will not handle this type of complaint, in which case you will have to take your case to small claims court, or, if the claim is more than the court's limit, to higher court. That, unfortunately, will mean higher costs, greater delays, and added complexity.

If your rental home has health or safety violations, notify your landlord in writing that you want them corrected. If nothing happens, notify the housing agency and include a copy of your letter to the landlord. Ask the agency to send an inspector to look at the property. The landlord can be fined for violations and, in some states, you can withhold rent until they are corrected.

In some states, tenants can even use the code violations to defend themselves against lawsuits for nonpayment of rent. If a court or rental housing agency rules that such a defense is valid, it can reduce the amount of rent the tenant owes.

RESOURCES

Books

Although many of the following books are written for landlords, the discussions and information can be useful to tenants in learning and enforcing their rights.

The Rights of Tenants. Richard E. Blumberg and James Grow. Avon Books, 105 Madison Ave., New York, NY 10016. (212) 481-5600. 1978 (out of print). 192 pages. $2.50.

A somewhat outdated source on tenants' legal rights. The book was written in association with the American Civil Liberties Union.

The Landlord's Law Book: Evictions. David Brown. Nolo Press, 950 Parker St., Berkeley, CA 94710. (415) 549-1976. 1986. 170 pages. $19.95.

A comprehensive manual on how to handle each step of an eviction and how to represent yourself in court.

The Landlord's Law Book: Rights and Responsibilities. David Brown and Ralph Warner. Nolo Press, 950 Parker St., Berkeley, CA 94710. (415) 549-1976. 1987. 175 pages. $24.95.

A comprehensive legal guide for landlords with sections on discrimination, insurance, tenants' privacy, leases, security deposits, rent control, liability, and rent withholding.

Landlord and Tenant Law. David S. Hill. West Publishing Co., P.O. Box 64526, St. Paul, MN 55164. (612) 228-2500. 1986. 311 pages. $10.95.

A compact format and reliable guide to the law for both students and lawyers. Uses legalese.

Landlords and Tenants: Your Guide to the Law. Scott Slonim. American Bar Association Press, 750 N. Lakeshore Dr., Chicago, IL 60611. (312) 988-5555. 1982. 48 pages. $3.

A short guide through landlord-tenant laws, giving a general understanding of the law. Useful glossary.

Organizations and Agencies

The U.S. Department of Housing and Urban Development (HUD).

This is the federal agency responsible for administering federal programs related to the nation's housing. HUD is divided into two sections: the Office of Fair Housing and Equal Opportunity and the Office of Neighborhoods, Voluntary Associations and Consumer Protection. The Office of Fair Housing is chiefly concerned with housing problems of lower-income and minority groups. The Office of Neighborhoods protects consumer interests in all housing and community-development activities. For information on available publications and services, contact the regional office near you. These are listed in Appendix IV.

National Housing Institute, 439 Main St., Orange, NJ 07050. (201) 678-3110.

This organization supports nationwide tenants' groups and is a resource for information on tenants' rights.

Legal Services Corporation (LSC), 400 Virginia Ave. SW, Washington, DC 20024. (202) 863-1820.

The LSC represents people who meet income guidelines in eviction cases and other landlord-tenant disputes. Call the national office, ask at your courthouse for a local referral, or check the government listings in your telephone directory.

The Tenants' Resource Center, 855 Grove St., Lansing, MI 48823. (517) 337-9795.

This is a Michigan-based organization whose pamphlets are valuable elsewhere, especially those on *Maintenance, Eviction,* and *Security Deposits.*

The National Housing Law Project, 122 C St. NW, Suite 220, Washington, DC 20001. (202) 783-5140.

This group, funded by LSC, is mainly a lawyer-training organization. It offers tenants a number of informational books and brochures. Write for a list.

CHAPTER 20

CONTRACT LANGUAGE

Most landlords use standard leases and "boilerplate" language usually weighted heavily in favor of the landlord. Some provisions may not even comply with laws that govern the landlord-tenant relationship.

Don't be afraid to bring to the landlord's attention any provisions that are illegal, or to modify them or strike them from the lease altogether. If you do sign a lease that has an illegal clause, that clause is void. A court will not enforce it, though the remainder of the lease will remain in effect.

Following is a standard lease for an unfurnished apartment. The traditional boilerplate language is followed by a plain-language translation and, where needed, an explanation and suggested alternative language to replace provisions unfair to tenants. The provisions included here are typical, though there are many variations. Your ability to negotiate the terms of your lease depends on your leverage with the landlord, but don't hesitate to try. In any case, *be sure to read your lease carefully* and to understand everything before signing it. (For purposes of this example, we assume you are the person renting the apartment.)

Made this _____ day of __*(month)*__ A.D. one thousand nine hundred and __*(year)*__ , by and between __*(landlord's name)*__ of __*(city, state)*__ , party of the first part, and _(your name)_ of _(city, state)_ , party of the second part.

Witnesseth, that the said party of the first part does let and demise unto the said party of the second part the following described premises: _(address, including apartment #, city, state)_ for the term of _(number of months or years)_ commencing on the _____ day of _(month, year)_ to the _____ day of _(month, year)_ for the sum of _(amount of rent per year)_ dollars per annum, payable in monthly installments of _(amount of rent per month)_ dollars, in advance and without demand, at _(address where rent is to be paid)_ , the first payment to be made on the _____ day of _(month, year)_ , and a like sum on the same day of each and every month thereafter.

This identifies the landlord and tenant, the property to be rented, the rental fee, where and when the rent must be paid, and the term of the contract. "Party of the first part" simply refers to the landlord, and "party of the second part" to you, the tenant.

Some leases include an "escalator clause" that allows the landlord to increase your rent to pass on any increased operating expenses. This one doesn't.

The word _demise_ means "rent" or "lease." With the words _without demand,_ the contract waives the landlord's obligation to notify you every month that your rent is due. This is standard.

Usually, once the term of the lease (one year, for instance) is up, you can move out or sign a new lease. The landlord can raise the rent at this time, within any limits set by rent-control laws, and both the landlord and you can renegotiate any terms of the lease.

1. This lease agreement is conditioned upon the party of the first part being able to secure possession of said premises from existing tenant, if any, by the commencement date hereof, and if party of the first part is unable to deliver posses-

sion of said premises to party of the second part by the commencement date hereof for any reason, such right of possession by party of the second part shall be postponed until such time when said premises shall be put in suitable physical condition for occupancy, or until such time when party of the first part is able to legally deliver possession, without any liability on the part of the party of the first part to the party of the second part for such postponement.

Bad news for tenants: This means that if the apartment isn't ready to move into, you have no recourse for getting your money back or canceling the lease. "Delivering possession" means turning over the premises, handing over the keys to the apartment. In some places, this clause is illegal. Here's some suggested alternative language:

1. If landlord is unable to deliver possession to tenant for any reason not within the landlord's control, tenant shall have the option of a) terminating this lease and recovering all money paid to landlord under this lease or b) having rent abated until possession can be given.

*   *   *

2. It is covenanted and agreed that the party of the second part has deposited with the party of the first part the sum of *(amount of monthly rent)* dollars, $ *(rent in numbers)* to be held by the party of the first part as security for the faithful performance of and compliance with all the terms, covenants and conditions of this lease. If the party of the second part fails to comply with each of said terms, covenants and conditions, the security shall belong to the party of the first part as part payment for the disbursements, attorneys' fees, costs and expenses that the party of the first part may undergo for the purpose of regaining possession of the premises and preparing same for renting; and no portion of said security deposit shall be used by the party of the second part for any payment of any rent due.

This requires you to pay the landlord a security deposit of one month's rent on signing the lease. In convoluted language, it states that if you break any conditions of this agreement, the landlord can withhold the security deposit to pay for legal or other expenses incurred in evicting you and renting the apartment to someone else. You are not allowed to use the security deposit for paying your rent for any month, including the last month of the lease.

Almost all states have laws that govern this security deposit, usually limiting the amount that can be charged, the time within which it must be returned, and the interest that must be returned with it.

Although the amount charged here is within the limit allowed by all jurisdictions (one month's rent), this is a bad clause for you because it allows the landlord to keep the entire deposit, even if your breach doesn't cost the landlord much money. Also, it doesn't specify any terms for returning the deposit to you. Although landlords may try to include language like this, most will agree to something a bit fairer. Here's an alternative plain-language provision:

2. On signing this agreement, tenant shall pay landlord *(amount spelled out) ($ amount in numbers),* as security. Such deposit, plus ___% interest per year, shall be returned to tenant within two weeks after the term has expired and tenants have vacated the premises. If all or part of the deposit is withheld, landlord must provide a written statement explaining why. Landlord may withhold only that part of the deposit necessary to: a) cover any unpaid rent; b) repair, at reasonable cost, any damage to the premises beyond normal wear and tear; or c) clean premises not left in the same condition as when tenant moved in. On tenant's request, landlord shall provide receipts for repairs paid for from the security deposit. Tenant shall not use the security deposit toward the payment of rent.

*　　　*　　　*

3. It is further covenanted and agreed by party of the second part that time is of the essence with regard to the payment of rent when due, and that a late payment charge of *(amount spelled out)* dollars *($ amount in numbers)* shall be paid for any check returned or received after the ___ day of the month.

This sets a late charge for rent that is not paid within a specified number of days of the due date. If a rent check is returned from the bank, it is considered late and a late fee is charged. As mentioned previously, many places have laws that limit late fees you can be charged or require a certain number of "grace" days before a landlord can charge this fee. Make sure the lease is in line with local laws.

> 4. It is covenanted and agreed that the said party of the second part, upon paying aforesaid rent and performing the covenants and conditions of this lease, shall and may peaceably and quietly have, hold and enjoy the demised premises for the term aforesaid.

This says you'll be entitled to the "quiet enjoyment" of the rental property. This is the most basic provision of your lease—it establishes your temporary possession of the rental property and your right to live there undisturbed. If this is not in your lease, most courts consider it an implied term by law.

> 5. It is further covenanted and agreed that the said party of the second part will not carry on any business therein nor use said premises for disorderly or unlawful purpose, nor in any noisy, boisterous or other manner offensive to any other occupant of the building; nor shall the party of the second part keep animals or birds of any description in said premises without the written consent of the party of the first part.

This is standard. It requires you to use the rental property only as a private residence and for no other purpose without the landlord's written consent in advance. The rest of the paragraph restricts you from using the property for any disruptive or illegal purpose, from keeping pets and from disturbing the peace and quiet of other tenants in the building by excessive noise or other activity. If the landlord agrees that you can keep a pet, cross out the last clause of the paragraph and be sure it is initialed by both the landlord and you.

For your protection, also add:

5A. Landlord agrees to prevent other tenants and other persons in the building or common areas from similarly disturbing tenant's peace and quiet.

* * *

6. It is further covenanted and agreed that the said party of the second part will pay the said rent as above stated, and all bills for gas and electricity used on the premises, making the necessary deposits at the respective offices to secure same, and that he/she will pay all water rents for said premises during his/her tenancy thereof.

This holds you responsible for paying all gas, electricity, and water charges. Some landlords charge a set fee for one or more utilities. You should know in advance exactly what utilities you will have to pay in addition to your rent. Cross out and initial those charges for which you are not responsible.

7. It is further covenanted and agreed that the party of the second part will conform to the rules and regulations made or hereafter made by the party of the first part for the management of the building, its corridors, porches, lobbies, drives, grounds and other appurtenances, and for the delivery of goods, merchandise and other things by tradespeople and other persons.

This requires that you agree to comply with the landlord's rules and regulations regarding management of the building, the grounds, and deliveries to the building. Check to see if you can get a copy of any rules and regulations before you move in.

8. It is further covenanted and agreed that the said party of the second part will keep said premises, including the building, fixtures, plumbing and appurtenances thereof, in substantial

condition and in good repair, clean, and in good working order and proper sanitary condition, all of which premises are now in such condition and repair; and that all repairs rendered necessary by the negligence of the party of the second part shall be paid for by him/her; and the said party of the second part will surrender the same at the expiration of said tenancy in good order, ordinary wear and tear and damage by the elements or public enemy excepted.

If you sign a lease that includes such language, you're acknowledging that the property, including the fixtures and plumbing, is clean and in good working condition. You're also agreeing to keep them that way, except for ordinary wear and tear. If you or people you allow into your apartment damage anything in it, you will be responsible for paying for repairs. That's why it's important to inspect the property first to make sure it is, in fact, in good condition. If it isn't, ask the landlord to fix any problems or note on the lease any existing damage before you move in. Otherwise you may wind up paying for it when you leave.

9. It is further covenanted and agreed that the said party of the second part will not make any alterations or additions to the structure, equipment or fixtures of said premises without written consent of the party of the first part first had and obtained.

Almost every lease contains this provision. It prevents you from making any alterations or additions without the landlord's prior written consent. If you do make changes without permission, the landlord may have the right to evict you and certainly will be able to charge for restoring the property to its original state, regardless of whether you believe you improved the property by your alterations.

10. It is further covenanted and agreed that the said party of the second part will permit the party of the first part free access at any time to the premises hereby leased for the purpose of examining or exhibiting the same, or in the event

of an emergency or fire or other property damage, or to make any repairs or alterations of such premises which said party of the first part considers necessary or desirable.

Beware: this allows the landlord to enter your apartment at *any time.* You should insist instead that visits by the landlord occur only between 9:00 A.M. and 5:00 P.M. (or suitable hours of your choosing) after 24 or 48 hours' notice, except in cases of serious emergency, such as fire.

11. It is further covenanted and agreed that all personal property in said premises shall be and remain at the sole risk of party of the second part, and party of the first part shall not be liable for any damage to, or loss of, such property arising from any acts of negligence of any other persons or from any other cause whatsoever, nor shall the party of the first part be liable for any injury to the party of the second part or other persons in or about the premises.

This may very well be illegal, at least in some situations. It exempts the landlord from responsibility for any loss or damage to your property or any personal injury to you or people you invite to the property, *regardless of who is at fault.* Such provisions have been ruled illegal when the landlord has the duty to maintain the property in a safe and sanitary condition and the damage or injury is the landlord's fault. Here's some suggested alternative language:

11. Tenant agrees to be liable for damage to tenant's personal property due to tenant's own negligence or that of others on the premises with tenant's permission. Tenant agrees to be liable for personal injury received on the premises by tenant or others on the premises with tenant's permission, due to their own negligence. Landlord shall maintain the building and grounds in a safe and sanitary condition, and comply with all state and local laws concerning the condition of dwelling units. Landlord shall take reasonable measures to maintain security on the premises, building and grounds to protect the tenant and those on the premises with tenant's permission from bur-

glary, robbery and other crimes. Tenant agrees to make use of such security measures as a reasonable person would.

12. It is further covenanted and agreed that the said party of the second part will not sublet said premises or any portion thereof or assign this lease in whole or in part without the consent in writing of said party of the first part.

This restricts you from subletting the apartment or assigning your lease before it expires. Ask the landlord to add the sentence:

12A. The landlord shall not unreasonably withhold consent.

13. It is further covenanted and agreed that if the said party of the second part shall fail to pay the said rent in advance as aforesaid, although there shall have been no legal or formal demand for the same, or shall neglect to pay the electricity or gas bills at the time and on the day when the same shall fall due and be payable as hereinbefore mentioned, or shall sublet or assign the said premises, or carry on any business therein without the written consent as aforesaid, or shall use the same for any disorderly or unlawful purpose, or break any of the aforesaid covenants, then, and in any of said events, this lease, and all things herein contained, shall cease, and the party of the first part, his/her heirs and assigns, shall be entitled to the possession of said leased premises, and to re-enter the same without demand, and may forthwith proceed to recover possession of said premises under and by virtue of the provisions of the law relating to proceedings in cases between party of the first part and party of the second part, any notice to quit or of intention to exercise said option, or to re-enter the premises being hereby waived by the party of the second part and assigns.

Watch out for this clause! While at first it might appear to simply repeat most of the earlier clauses of the lease to define what will constitute a breach by you, the end of the clause is the real kicker. It defines the landlord's rights if you break the lease. Here, the landlord would have the immediate right to enter the apartment without notice and to institute legal proceedings to evict you. It also waives your right to receive notice that the rent is overdue or that the apartment must be vacated.

As discussed previously, the waivers in this lease are illegal in many states. It is usually illegal to require you to waive your right to receive notice of eviction proceedings. A landlord may also include language by which you waive other rights, such as the right to a jury trial in disputes over the lease. If the waiver is illegal, the clause will not be enforced by a court if the landlord ever tries to take advantage of it.

However, it's best to be prudent and strike through such language. If it isn't crossed out, a court may hold you to it if it decides you knowingly and voluntarily signed the lease and all its provisions.

We suggest splitting this paragraph into two, because the legal remedies available to landlords when a tenant hasn't paid the rent may be different from those used when a tenant breaks other conditions of the lease. Here's our suggested alternate language:

> 13. If tenant fails to comply with a provision of this lease, other than to pay rent, landlord shall notify tenant of such breach and allow tenant reasonable time to correct the problem. If tenant does not do so, landlord may terminate this agreement as provided by law.
>
> 13A. If tenant is unable to pay rent when due and notifies landlord on or before that date of an inability to do so, landlord and tenant shall make reasonable efforts to work out a procedure for tenant to pay rent as soon as possible. If they are unable to do so, landlord may serve notice to pay rent or vacate, as provided by law.
>
> *   *   *
>
> 14. It is further covenanted and agreed that no waiver of one breach of any covenant herein shall be construed to be a waiver of the covenant itself, or of subsequent breach thereof or of this agreement; and if any breach occurs and afterwards is adjusted, this lease shall continue in full force as if no breach had occurred.

This complicated language is best explained by example. Say you sublet the apartment without the landlord's consent and the landlord, upon discovering this, decides it's okay for the subtenant to stay (in other words, *waives* your *breach*). The landlord's waiver does not mean you may again sublet without the landlord's consent, nor does it mean the landlord waives your other obligations under the lease.

15. It is further covenanted and agreed that, should party of the second part continue in possession after the end of the term herein, with permission of the party of the first part, any such holding over shall be construed as a tenancy from month-to-month at the same monthly rental as hereinabove provided as the monthly installment and such tenancy shall be subject to all the terms, conditions, covenants and agreements of this lease, except that nothing in this paragraph shall preclude party of the first part from increasing the rent at any time after the expiration of the term of this lease.

16. It is further covenanted and agreed that the party of the second part shall provide at least thirty (30) days' written notice to party of the first part of his/her intention to either renew, extend or terminate this lease upon its expiration, or upon the expiration of any renewal or extension thereof, although party of the first part shall be under no obligation to renew or extend this lease beyond its stated term.

These are renewal provisions. This lease has a *holding over* provision that automatically renews the lease month-to-month at the end of the first term. Here, the renewal is also subject to the landlord's agreement that you stay. Finally, it allows the landlord to raise your rent anytime after the original lease term expires. The second provision simply says you must give the landlord 30 days' written notice before moving out.

17. It is further covenanted and agreed that the party of the second part shall pay and discharge all costs, expenses and attorneys' fees which shall be incurred and expended by the

party of the first part in enforcing the covenants and agreements of this lease, whether by the institution of litigation or in the taking of advice of counsel, or otherwise.

This makes you responsible for paying all legal expenses the landlord incurs in enforcing the conditions of the lease, including litigation and seeking a lawyer's advice. It is obviously one-sided. In some areas it is illegal to require you to pay your landlord's legal fees. We suggest that either you each pay your own legal fees or use this alternative language:

17. If either party initiates a legal proceeding to enforce any provision of this lease, the successful party shall collect reasonable attorneys' fees and costs from the other.

In testimony whereof, the said parties have hereunto signed their names and affixed their seals, this _____ day of _(month, year)_ .

(landlord's signature) for _(Company, if any) (date)_ (seal)

(tenant's signature) _(date)_ (seal)

Witnessed by:

(witness's name)

(signature) (seal)

The lease is not binding until it is signed. Seals and witnesses are not necessary, however. The lease will be valid without them.

PART VII

LESSER CONTRACTS

CHAPTER 21

RELEASES

E*ric slips and falls in front of an apartment building and sprains his ankle. The owner of the building agrees to pay his medical expenses if Eric signs an agreement not to sue.*

Ira is injured in a train collision. The company's lawyer visits him in the hospital and asks him to sign a paper giving up his right to sue in exchange for $5,000.

Releases like these are among the most common do-it-yourself contracts people sign. Because they are brief and straightforward, it isn't difficult to write your own and make them legally binding without a lawyer's help.

In a *release,* one person agrees to pay another to surrender a legal claim. Usually, releases are used to settle small claims, such as those for minor damages from "fender bender" auto accidents. For example, after the other driver admits fault for the "fender bender," in exchange for a small sum of money you may agree not to report the accident to your insurance company and not to sue. If you write down the agreement and sign it, you have created a contract called a release: One side "releases" or gives up an otherwise valid claim.

As explained in Chapter 1, all contracts, including releases, must involve consideration. This means the person who signs the release must receive something in exchange for giving up a legal right or claim. If you sign a release surrendering your right to sue your friend for a back injury you received at her house but get nothing in return from her, the release is void. You have made no exchange to support the contract. If related back problems arise later, you are legally free to sue for damages.

Although money is a common consideration for a release, it's not the only kind. For example, if your cousin seeds your lawn for $400 and the grass fails to grow, she may ask you to drop all legal claims in exchange for redoing the lawn work until the grass grows. If you agree, that's a legal release.

In general, a release is valid if both sides understand the terms and sign voluntarily. If one side later challenges the release, the court will not void the release unless it finds convincing evidence of duress, coercion, or "unconscionability" (see Chapter 1).

GENERAL AND SPECIFIC

Both the releases in our examples were *specific,* based on a particular incident and affecting the outcome of only one incident. Your situation may require a *general* release, however. You may, for example, give up all claims against a relative's estate or against a doctor for medical malpractice in exchange for a sum of money. General releases usually include language like: "For $5,000, I give up any and all legal claims I might have against you, up to and including the date this release is signed."

READ CAREFULLY

Signing away your right to sue can have significant consequences. It's important that you fully understand the value of the claim you are giving up. If you are signing a release that says you won't sue for damages from an injury, be certain you know the full extent of your injuries. Consider getting a medical opinion or two before you sign the release.

Fully assess both the potential gains and costs of settling a claim with a release. Remember, going to court means you'll probably have to pay lawyers' fees, and it may be a long time before the case is decided and you can collect. Further, you'll risk losing the case. On the other hand, when you surrender a claim in exchange for a quick and certain resolution, the amount you'll get will almost surely be less that what you might get in court, if you win.

The following is a hypothetical general release written in legalese, followed by its translation.

RELEASE

I, *(releasor)* , for and in consideration of the sum of _____ in hand paid by *(releasee)*, have remised, released, and forever discharged by these presents for my heirs, executors and administrators remise, release and forever discharge his/her heirs, executors and administrators of and from any and all matter of action and actions, cause and causes of action, suits, debts, dues, sums of money, accounts, reckonings, bonds, bills, specialties, covenants, contracts, controversies, agreements, premises, variances, trespasses, damages, judgments, extents, executions, claims and demand whatsoever, in law or in equity against which I ever had, now have, or which my heirs, executors or administrators hereafter can, shall, or may have, for, upon or by reason of any matter, cause or thing whatsoever, from the beginning of the world to the day of the date of these presents.

_____	_____
Releasor's Signature	*Date*
_____	_____
Releasee's Signature	*Date*

In Witness Whereof, I, _____ have hereunto set hand and seal the ___ day of _____ one thousand nine hundred and ___.

Sealed and delivered in the presence of:

<u>*(notary's signature)*</u>
Notary Public

Translation.   This is a general release in language that is both repetitive and unnecessarily complex. It says that for a sum of money, you, the *releasor,* forever give up any right to sue the *releasee* for any legal claims that are based on any event that occurred before the agreement is signed. It also says that your heirs can't sue the releasee or the releasee's heirs.

This agreement also includes the unnecessary notarization (see Chapter 1). Witnesses are not necessary; they do not affect the validity of the contract, although if you foresee a possible challenge to the contract, consider having witnesses sign. Both releasor and releasee, of course, must sign and date the contract.

The only difference between this general release and a specific release is that, instead of including the words "giving up any and all claims up to and until this date," a specific release would state: "giving up any and all claims" that arise from the specific incident, for instance "a car accident at Penn and First Streets in Middleburg" on a certain date.

Here's a release written in plain language:

PLAIN LANGUAGE RELEASE

This Release, dated _____, is given:
By the releasor(s)   <u>*(your name and address),*</u> referred to as "I", to the Releasee(s)   <u>*(name and address),*</u> referred to as "You."

If more than one person signs this Release, "I" shall mean each person who signs this Release as a releasor.

1. **Release:** I release and give up any and all claims and rights which I may have against you, including those of which I am not aware.

2. **Consideration:** I, the releasor, have received good and adequate consideration for this release in the form of <u>*(what is exchanged for the release).*</u>

3. Who is Bound: I am bound by this Release. Anyone who succeeds to my rights and responsibilities, such as my heirs or the executor of my estate, is also bound. This Release is made for your benefit and all who succeed to your rights and responsibilities, such as your heirs or the executor of your estate.

_____   _____
Releasor's Signature   *Date*

_____   _____
Releasee's Signature   *Date*

In community property states, spouses' signatures are also required if any joint property is affected.

CHAPTER 22

POWERS OF ATTORNEY

Sally is terminally ill and concerned about who will make health decisions should she become mentally unable to. She wants to put her sister in charge and put it in writing.

A *power of attorney* is a contract that permits another person to act on your behalf. It must be in writing. People generally use a power of attorney to allow someone else to handle one or more of their business transactions—paying bills, withdrawing money from a bank, selling or buying a house, even making investments. For example, you might authorize someone (called your *agent* or *attorney in fact*) to sell your car while you are on vacation.

CONVENTIONAL POWERS OF ATTORNEY

Limited Power of Attorney
To designate someone to act on your behalf for one or more specific business transactions, use a *limited* or *conventional* power of attorney.

Unlimited Power of Attorney
You can also use a power of attorney to authorize someone to handle all your business decisions. This is done by a *general* or *unlimited* power of attorney. These come in

handy any time you're away from home, in the military, temporarily relocated overseas for your job, or away on vacation, but people use them to grant authority even while they stay in the area. An unlimited power of attorney gives the person you choose the power to make all necessary financial and other business decisions.

DURABLE POWER OF ATTORNEY

A *durable power of attorney* authorizes someone to make medical and/or financial decisions for you if you become physically or mentally unable to make them. For example, if you're ill, you might give a durable power of attorney to a family member or friend who would sign checks, pay bills, and take charge of your financial affairs. A durable power of attorney can be limited or unlimited.

A durable power of attorney remains effective *when you become incapacitated,* and removes the need for a court to step in and appoint a *guardian* or *conservator* because you have already made that assignment. You can write one that becomes effective *only* when you become incapacitated.

CONSUMER TIPS

Find a Trustworthy Agent.   Because a power of attorney transfers considerable responsibility and power over your affairs, caution is advised. Only give your power of attorney to someone whose honesty and business judgment you fully trust.

Use a Limited Power of Attorney If Possible.   It's best to transfer the least amount of responsibility and power over your financial or medical affairs to another. You can do this best with a limited power of attorney. If you are creating a general or durable power of attorney, be particularly careful whom you entrust with this responsibility.

Powers of Attorney Can be Canceled at Any Time. It's important to know that you can cancel the power of attorney at any time, with one exception: if it is a durable power of attorney and the court considers you incapacitated. To revoke a power of attorney, simply prepare a second document that states you are revoking it. This is true even if you do not have a clause about revocation in the original power of attorney.

Set an Expiration Date. It's a good idea to include a date on which the power of attorney will expire, whether the contract is general or limited. Even if you're leaving town to care for an ailing parent and don't know how long you'll be gone, choose a date. If the power of attorney is needed after the expiration date, you can always execute another one. This date protects you from the power of attorney being misused after it has been revoked.

Check for Required Forms. The Internal Revenue Service (IRS), banks, and other institutions sometimes have specific power-of-attorney forms they want you to use. In some cases, they may refuse to acknowledge a power of attorney not completed on their form. Make sure you complete the correct form for the uses you anticipate.

You Don't Need a Notary Public. You don't need to get your power of attorney notarized, although notarizing it doesn't make the agreement any less valid.

Notify People and Institutions When You Give or Revoke Your Power of Attorney. Be sure you give a copy of your power of attorney to anyone who'll be affected. For instance, if you're giving someone a power of attorney to withdraw money and write checks on your bank account, send the bank a copy. Later, if you revoke the power of attorney, send the bank a copy of the revocation as well.

Following are a limited power of attorney and a plain-language durable power of attorney:

LIMITED POWER OF ATTORNEY

I, _____ hereby appoint _____, my true and lawful attorney for me and authorize her/him in my name to demand payment of claims to become due for _____ located at _____, and to give releases of discharges for the same, also to perform and execute those things which she/he deems necessary for the carrying on of said business.

Signature	*Date*

Translation. This power of attorney is "limited" because it appoints someone only to handle the transactions of a specific business, named in the document. For example, under this power of attorney the agent can pay employees' salaries and buy whatever the business requires, but not withdraw money from a personal banking account or handle any matters not related to the named business.

DURABLE POWER OF ATTORNEY FOR HEALTH CARE AND FINANCIAL/ASSET MANAGEMENT

1. Creation of Durable Power of Attorney

To all those concerned or involved with my finances/assets and/or health care, including my family, relatives, friends and my physicians, health care providers, community care facilities and any other person who may have an interest or duty in my medical care or treatment: I, _____, being of sound mind, intentionally and voluntarily intend to create by this document a durable power of attorney for my health care and the management of my finances and assets, by appointing as the person designated as my attorney in fact to make health care decisions for me and manage my finances and assets for me in the event I become incapacitated and am unable to make health care decisions or manage my finances and assets myself. This power of attorney shall not be affected by my subsequent incapacity.

This paragraph establishes that you, the writer, declare that you are of sound mind and voluntarily create this durable power of attorney. It transfers authority for health-care decisions and financial and asset management, but becomes effective only if you become incapacitated and unable to make health-care and financial decisions for yourself.

2. Designation of Attorney in Fact
The person designated to be my attorney in fact for health care and financial/asset management in the event I become incapacitated is _____ of _____. If _____ for any reason shall fail to serve or ceases to serve as my attorney in fact, _____ of _____ shall be my attorney in fact for health care and financial/asset management.

This paragraph names the agent or attorney in fact and, if that person cannot act as the agent, also names a replacement or second choice.

3. Effective on Incapacity
This durable power of attorney shall become effective in the event I become incapacitated and am unable to make health care decisions for myself and/or manage my own finances/ assets, in which case it shall become effective as of the date of the written statement by a physician, as provided in Paragraph 4.

This document becomes effective only upon the writer's incapacity and inability to make health-care decisions and decisions about managing finances and assets. It becomes effective on the date a doctor issues a written statement of incapacity, as provided in the two next paragraphs.

4. Determination of Incapacity
(A) The determination that I have become incapacitated and am unable to make health care decisions for myself and/or am unable to manage my finances/assets shall be made in writing

by a licensed physician. If possible, the physician shall be
_____ of _____.
(B) In the event that a licensed physician has made a written
determination that I have become incapacitated and am not
able to make health care decisions for myself and/or am unable to manage my finances/assets, that written statement
shall be attached to the original document of this power of
attorney.

This section provides that a licensed doctor must make
the determination of incapacity, and that the determination
must be put in writing. The author of this power of attorney
also names the doctor who is to make the determination, if
possible, and requires that the written statement of incapacity be attached to the original power of attorney.

5. Authority for My Attorney in Fact over Health Care Decisions
(A) Authority in General
My attorney in fact shall have all lawful authority permissi-
ble to make health care decisions for me, including the
authority to consent or withdraw consent or refuse consent to any care, treatment, service or procedure to maintain, diagnose or treat my physical or mental condition,
EXCEPT:

Here the writer should enter any desired limitations or
directions for the attorney in fact, such as:

(A.1) No life support systems shall be used to artificially pro-
long my life if I have an incurable disease.
*   *   *
(B) Authority for Inspection and Disclosure of Information
Relating to My Physical or Mental Health
Subject to any limitations in this document, my attorney
in fact has the power and authority to do all of the following:
(1) Request, review, and receive any information, verbal
or written, regarding my physical or mental health,

including, but not limited to, medical and hospital records.

(2) Execute on my behalf any releases or other document that may be required in order to obtain this information.

(3) Consent to the disclosure of this information.

(C) Authority to Sign Documents, Waivers and Releases
When necessary to implement the health care decisions that my attorney in fact is authorized by this document to make, my attorney in fact has the power and authority to execute on my behalf all of the following:

(1) Documents titled or purporting to be a "Refusal To Permit Treatment" and "Leaving Hospital Against Medical Advice."

(2) Any necessary waiver or release from liability required by a hospital or physician.

This defines the agent's authority over health-care decisions. In this example, the scope is wide and includes consenting to or refusing any treatment or medication. This is the place to make exceptions or prohibitions, however. Here, for example, you might state that you do not want to use artificial life support systems; your agent would then be forbidden to order such treatment for you.

The agent is also given access to all information and records on your physical and mental health. To carry out health care decisions, the agent has your authority to execute on your behalf any necessary waivers or releases and documents, such as a "Refusal To Permit Treatment."

6. Authority of My Attorney in Fact to Manage My Finances/ Assets

(A) Except as specified in Section 6(B), I grant my attorney in fact full power and authority over all my property, real and personal, and authorize him/her to do and perform all and every act which I as an owner of said property could do or perform, and I hereby ratify and confirm all that my attorney in fact shall do or cause to be done under this durable power of attorney.

(B) My attorney in fact has no authority to give any of my property to himself/herself.

This defines the attorney in fact's authority over your finances and assets. It gives unlimited power over all real and personal property, with only one restriction: The attorney in fact may not make your property his or her own. This sensible restriction makes clear that the agent is not free to manipulate finances for personal benefit.

7. Reliance by Third Parties
The powers conferred on my attorney in fact by this durable power of attorney and my attorney in fact's signature or act under the authority granted in this durable power of attorney may be accepted by any third person or organization as fully authorized by me and with the same force and effect as if I were personally present, competent and acting on my own behalf.
   No person or organization who relies on this durable power of attorney or any representation my attorney in fact makes regarding his or her authority, including but not limited to:
(1) The fact that this durable power of attorney has not been revoked;
(2) That I, *(your name)* was competent to execute this power of attorney;
(3) The authority of my attorney in fact under this durable power of attorney;
shall incur any liability to me, my estate, heirs, successors or assigns because of such reliance on this durable power of attorney or on any such representation by my attorney in fact.

All third parties are notified by this language that the agent alone has full authority to act on your behalf. A third party will never be held liable for any action the third party takes because he or she relied on the validity of the document.

8. Duration
I intend that this Durable Power of Attorney remain effective

until my death, or until revoked by me in writing.
Executed this _____ day of _____ at _____.

*(your name)*_____
Principal

*(witness's name)*_____   *(witness's name)*_____
Witness   Witness

This durable power of attorney will remain in effect until
the author revokes it or dies. It's best to have it signed by
at least two witnesses, although the exact number needed
varies according to state law. The attorney in fact need not
sign a power of attorney for it to be valid.

CHAPTER 23

PROMISSORY NOTES

Your brother Bill agrees to sell you his stereo for $300. You agree to pay him your next paycheck. You decide you want the agreement in writing so he doesn't change his mind and sell it to his girlfriend.

Promissory notes like this one are usually loans between family members or friends. These loans are not regulated, like bank or lending-institution loans. In fact, the only laws that apply to promissory notes are usury laws: They restrict the interest the lender can charge. Promissory notes can be used for secured loans, but they are most often used for those that are unsecured.

You might use a promissory note when you loan your daughter money to make a down payment on a new car. It would include the amount of the loan, the repayment date and any interest owed, as well as your signatures. A promissory note might set up the installment payment plan to buy a stereo from someone who advertised in your local newspapers.

Promissory notes can be written so that the amount borrowed is payable in a *lump sum* or in smaller *installments*. The method of payment you choose depends on your circumstances. If you're the lender, you may want the right to transfer the note to a third person who will be able to collect the debt for you if you move, become incapacitated, or die.

To sell or transfer a promissory note simply by signing it over, like a check, it must be *negotiable*. That means it must include:

* The names and addresses of both the lender and borrower
* Language making the debt payable to the lender
* A specific sum to be paid and the interest rate, if any
* The address to which payments must be made
* The date and city where the note is signed
* The signature of the borrower

Promissory notes may also be assigned. See Chapter 24 for advice on drawing up an assignment contract.

Two negotiable, unsecured, plain-language promissory notes follow. The first is an agreement for a lump-sum repayment, the second for repayment in installments.

NEGOTIABLE PROMISSORY NOTE FOR A LUMP SUM

$_____

Ninety days after today's date, or on the _____ day of _____, or on demand, I promise (or we jointly promise) to pay _____ or bearer, _____ with ____% interest, for value received.

_____   _____
Borrower's Signature   *Witness*

PROMISSORY NOTE FOR INSTALLMENT PAYMENTS

$_____

On or before _____ for value received, I promise to pay _____ the sum of _____ dollars, with ____% interest. I agree to make monthly payments on the _____ day of each month for _____ months in the amount of _____ with the first payment due _____.

_____   _____
Borrower's Signature   *Witness*

CHAPTER 24

ASSIGNMENTS

Kevin's *brother Richard owes him $500 that is reflected in the promissory note they signed a year ago. Kevin lives 3,000 miles away in New York, and all his attempts to collect have been ignored by Richard. Their sister, Lisa, is going to visit Richard. Kevin decides to assign the note to Lisa for $400. Lisa will collect and earn $100 profit.*

You use an *assignment* to transfer to someone else a debt that's owed to you. For example, suppose you've sold your car and received a promissory note for $300 a month, but you want the money paid directly to your parents. You *assign* your promissory note to them. This means you've given your parents your *interest* in the money from the car sale. You no longer can personally collect the debt.

An assignment is exchanged for consideration—something of value. You might assign someone your promissory note in exchange for money. Say, for example, you hold a $1,000 promissory note payable in a year and you suddenly find you need money immediately. Your friend agrees to give you $900 now in exchange for the note. The friend makes a $100 profit, and you get $900 without having to wait the year.

You can assign virtually any definable interest you own. In addition to debts owed to you, you can assign your wages, your *accounts receivable,* your rights under a contract, even an expected inheritance. Although you cannot assign your right to sue (a court would rule that the person you assigned it to would have no legal right to sue because that person was not the one with a claim), you may assign your rights under a lawsuit already in progress.

Three sample assignment contracts follow. The first is a standard form in legalese, the second is a plain-language assignment of a promissory note, and the third is a plain-language assignment of a contract. You may choose to have the contract witnessed and notarized. Although the contract is no less valid if it is not witnessed, it may be easier to withstand a challenge if you have someone who can testify it was signed by both parties.

ASSIGNMENT OF A PARTICULAR ACCOUNT

_____ of _____, herein referred to as assignor, in consideration for _____, receipt whereof is hereby acknowledged, assigns to _____ of _____, his/her executors, administrators, and assigns, herein referred to as assignee, to his/her or their own proper use and benefit, all assignor's right, title, and interest in and to any and all sum or sums of money now due or to become due on the attached, or sales, services, loans, or whatever transaction may be the basis of the account. Assignor gives to assignee, his/her executors, administrators, and assigns, the full power and authority, for assignee's own use and benefit, but at assignee's own cost, to ask, demand, collect, receive, compound, and give acquittance for the same, or any part thereof, and in assignor's name or otherwise, to prosecute and withdraw any suits or proceedings at law or in equity therefore.

_____   _____
Signature   *Dated*

You, as the *assignor,* give the account entirely to the *assignee.* The heirs (the people who will inherit at death) of both of you are also bound by this agreement. Every right or claim, including money and services owed, is given to the assignee.

If any lawsuits are transferred with the assignment, the assignee owns the suit and can continue it or not, as he or she wishes.

PLAIN-LANGUAGE ASSIGNMENT
OF A PROMISSORY NOTE

For _____ received, I, _____, of _____, assign to _____, of _____, all of my rights to the promissory note dated _____, payable to my order on demand in the face amount of _____ and executed by _____.

In witness whereof, I have executed this assignment at _____.

_____
Signature

With this assignment, you have transferred to the assignee all rights to a promissory note that's owed to you by another person. The promissory note is identified by the amount, the date, and the people who signed it.

GENERAL ASSIGNMENT OF A CONTRACT

In consideration of _____ , I, _____, assign and transfer to _____ all rights and interest that I have or would have in the attached contract, called *(name of contract)* between *(the other party to the contract being assigned)* and me, subject to all its conditions and terms, and in so doing release and quit claim to all rights that I have or would have to receive property under that contract.

_____   _____
Name   *Signature*

_____   _____
Name   *Signature*

_____
Date

In this assignment, you, as the assignor, have transferred to someone else, your assignee, all your rights under a contract. Both of you sign the agreement. The contract that's being assigned is attached to this assignment and is also identified by naming it and the other party who signed the contract with you. You also state that you give up all your rights and claims under the contract and that the assignee accepts all those rights and claims.

APPENDIXES

CONSUMER PROTECTION AGENCIES

Consumer Protection Agencies resolve individual complaints against businesses and educate consumers and businesses about the law. They also provide information about consumer complaints filed against businesses in their area of jurisdiction. Some are operated by the state government, others by local governments.

To file a complaint, call the nearest office listed below and ask if your complaint needs to be in writing and on a particular form or if you can report it over the telephone. Some offices may ask you to come in for an interview. State offices may refer you to a local or county office. The information in this appendix is excerpted from the 1990 edition of the *Consumer's Resource Handbook,* published by the U.S. Office of Consumer Affairs.

Alabama
Consumer Protection Division
Office of Attorney General
11 S. Union St.
Montgomery, AL 36130
(205) 261-7334
(800) 392-5658 (toll free in AL)

Alaska
Consumer Protection Section
Office of Attorney General
1031 W. 4th Ave., Suite 110-B
Anchorage, AK 99501
(907) 279-0428

Arizona

Financial Fraud Division
Office of Attorney General
1275 W. Washington St.
Phoenix, AZ 85007
(602) 542-3702
(800) 352-8431 (toll free in AZ)

Arkansas

Consumer Protection Division
Office of Attorney General
200 Tower Bldg., 4th & Center
  Sts.
Little Rock, AR 72201
(501) 682-2007
(800) 482-8982 (toll free in AR)

California

Public Inquiry Unit
Office of Attorney General
1515 K St., Suite 511
Sacramento, CA 94244-2550
(916) 322-3360
(800) 952-5225 (toll free in CA)

Consumer Protection Division
Los Angeles City Attorney's
  Office
200 N. Main St.
1600 City Hall East
Los Angeles, CA 90012
(213) 485-4515

Colorado

Consumer Protection Unit
Office of Attorney General
1525 Sherman St., 3rd Floor
Denver, CO 80203
(303) 866-5167

Connecticut

Department of Consumer
  Protection
165 Capitol Ave.
Hartford, CT 06106
(203) 566-4999
(800) 842-2649 (toll free in CT)

Delaware

Division of Consumer Affairs
Department of Community
  Affairs
820 N. French St., 4th Floor
Wilmington, DE 19801
(302) 571-3250

District of Columbia

Department of Consumer &
  Regulatory Affairs
614 H St. NW
Washington, DC 20001
(202) 727-7000

Florida

Division of Consumer Services
218 Mayo Bldg.
Tallahassee, FL 32399
(904) 488-2226
(800) 342-2176 (toll free in FL)

Georgia

Governor's Office of Consumer
  Affairs
2 Martin Luther King, Jr. Dr.
  SE
Plaza Level, E. Tower
Atlanta, GA 30334
(404) 656-7000
(800) 282-5808 (toll free in
  GA)

Hawaii

Office of Consumer Protection
828 Fort St. Mall
Honolulu, HI 96812-3767
(808) 548-2560/2540

Idaho

None

Illinois

Consumer Protection Division
Office of Attorney General
100 W. Randolph St., 12th
  Floor
Chicago, IL 60601
(312) 917-3580

Indiana

Consumer Protection Division
Office of Attorney General
219 State House
Indianapolis, IN 46204
(317) 232-6330
(800) 382-5516 (toll free in IN)

Iowa

Consumer Protection Division
Office of Attorney General
1300 E. Walnut St., 2nd Floor
Des Moines, IA 50319
(515) 281-5926

Kansas

Consumer Protection Division
Office of Attorney General
Kansas Judicial Ctr., 2nd Floor
Topeka, KS 66612
(913) 296-3751
(800) 432-2310 (toll free in KS)

Kentucky

Consumer Protection Division
Office of Attorney General
209 St. Clair St.
Frankfort, KY 40601
(502) 564-2200
(800) 432-9257 (toll free in KY)

Louisiana

Consumer Protection Section
Office of Attorney General
State Capitol Bldg., P.O. Box
  94005
Baton Rouge, LA 70804
(504) 342-7013

Maine

Consumer and Antitrust
  Division
Office of Attorney General
State House Station #6
Augusta, ME 04333
(207) 289-3716 (9:00 A.M.–2:00
  P.M.)

Maryland

Consumer Protection Division
Office of Attorney General
7 N. Calvert St., 3rd Floor
Baltimore, MD 21202
(301) 528-8662 (9:00 A.M.–2:00
  P.M.)

Massachusetts

Consumer Protection Division
Office of Attorney General
One Ashburton Place, Room
  1411
Boston, MA 02108
(617) 727-7780

Michigan

Consumer Protection Division
Office of Attorney General
670 Law Bldg.
Lansing, MI 48913
(517) 373-1140

Minnesota

Office of Consumer Services
Office of Attorney General
117 University Ave.
St. Paul, MN 55155
(612) 296-2331

Mississippi

Consumer Protection Division
Office of Attorney General
P.O. Box 220
Jackson, MS 39205
(601) 359-3680

Missouri

Trade Offense Division
Office of Attorney General
P.O. Box 899
Jefferson City, MO 65102
(314) 751-2616
(800) 392-8222 (toll free in MO)

Montana

Consumer Affairs Unit
Department of Commerce
1424 9th Ave.
Helena, MT 59620
(406) 444-4312

Nebraska

Consumer Protection Division
Department of Justice
2115 State Capitol, P.O. Box 98920
Lincoln, NE 68509
(402) 471-4723

Nevada

Department of Commerce
State Mail Room Complex
Las Vegas, NV 89158
(702) 486-4150

New Hampshire

Consumer Protection and Antitrust Division
Office of Attorney General
State House Annex
Concord, NH 03301
(603) 271-3641

New Jersey

Division of Consumer Affairs
1100 Raymond Blvd., Room 504
Newark, NJ 07102
(201) 648-4010

New Mexico

Consumer and Economic Crime Division
Office of Attorney General
P.O. Box Drawer 1508
Santa Fe, NM 87504
(505) 872-6910
(800) 432-2070 (toll free in NM)

New York

Consumer Protection Board
99 Washington Ave.
Albany, NY 12210
(518) 474-8583

Consumer Protection Board
250 Broadway, 17th Floor
New York, NY 10007-2593
(212) 587-4908

North Carolina

Consumer Protection Section
Office of Attorney General
P.O. Box 629
Raleigh, NC 27602
(919) 733-7741

North Dakota

Consumer Fraud Division
Office of Attorney General
State Capitol Bldg.
Bismarck, ND 58505
(701) 224-2210
(800) 472-2600 (toll free in ND)

Ohio

Consumer Frauds and Crimes Section
Office of Attorney General
30 E. Broad St., 25th Floor
Columbus, OH 43266-0410
(614) 466-4986
(800) 282-0515 (toll free in OH)

Oklahoma

Consumer Affairs
Office of Attorney General
112 State Capitol Bldg.
Oklahoma City, OK 73105
(405) 521-3921

Oregon

Financial Fraud Section
Office of Attorney General
Justice Bldg.
Salem, OR 97310
(503) 378-4320

Pennsylvania

Bureau of Consumer Protection
Office of Attorney General
Strawberry Sq., 14th Floor
Harrisburg, PA 17120
(717) 787-9707
(800) 441-2555 (toll free in PA)

Puerto Rico

Department of Consumer Affairs
Minillas Station
P.O. Box 41059
Santurce, PR 00940
(809) 722-7555

Rhode Island

Consumer Protection Division
Department of Attorney General
72 Pine St.
Providence, RI 02903
(401) 277-2104
(800) 852-7776 (toll free in RI)

South Carolina

Department of Consumer Affairs
P.O. Box 5757
Columbia, SC 29250
(803) 734-9452
(800) 922-1594 (toll free in SC)

South Dakota

Division of Consumer Affairs
Office of Attorney General
State Capitol Bldg.
Pierre, SD 57501
(605) 773-4400

Tennessee

Division of Consumer Affairs
Department of Commerce &
  Insurance
500 James Robertson Pkwy.,
  5th Floor
Nashville, TN 37219
(615) 741-4737
(800) 342-8385 (toll free in
  TN)

Texas

Consumer Protection Division
Office of Attorney General
Box 12548, Capitol Station
Austin, TX 78711
(512) 463-2070

Utah

Division of Consumer
  Protection
Department of Business
  Regulation
160 E. Third South
P. O. Box 45802
Salt Lake City, UT 84145
(801) 530-6601

Vermont

Public Protection Division
Office of Attorney General
109 State St.
Montpelier, VT 05602
(802) 828-3171

Virgin Islands

Department of Licensing and
  Consumer Affairs
Property and Procurement
  Bldg.
Subbase #1, Room 205
St. Thomas, VI 0801
(809) 774-3130

Virginia

Division of Consumer Counsel
Office of Attorney General
Supreme Court Bldg.
101 N. 8th St.
Richmond, VA 23219
(804) 786-2116

Washington

Consumer and Business Fair
  Practices Division
710-2nd Ave., Suite 1300
Seattle, WA 98104
(206) 464-7744
(800) 551-4636 (toll free in
  WA)

West Virginia

Consumer Protection Division
Office of Attorney General
812 Quarrier St., 6th Floor
Charleston, WV 25301
(304) 348-8986
(800) 368-8808 (toll free in
  WV)

Wisconsin

Office of Consumer Protection
Department of Justice
P.O. Box 7856
Madison, WE 53707
(608) 266-1852
(800) 362-8189 (toll free in WI)

Wyoming

Office of Attorney General
123 State Capitol Bldg.
Cheyenne, WY 82002
(307) 777-6286

BETTER BUSINESS BUREAUS

$\mathbf{B}$etter Business Bureaus (BBBs) are private dispute-resolution centers funded by local businesses. They attempt to resolve problems between consumers and businesses informally. BBBs accept written complaints and try to get the two sides to reach agreement, through either mediation or arbitration.

BBBs handle problems with contractors, large and small; retailers; auto repair shops; and others. They also publish pamphlets on consumer issues and maintain records of the number of complaints filed against local companies. If you have doubts about any local business, call to ask how many complaints have been filed against it. Also ask about the proper form to use before sending in a complaint. The information in this appendix is excerpted from the 1990 edition of the *Consumer's Resource Handbook,* published by the U.S. Office of Consumer Affairs.

If your state is not listed below, call the national office.

National Headquarters
Council of Better Business
  Bureaus
4200 Wilson Blvd.
Arlington, VA 22203
(703) 276-0100

Local Bureaus

Alabama
1214 S. 20th St.
Birmingham, AL 35205
(205) 558-2222

P. O. Box 383
Huntsville, AL 35804
(205) 533-1640

707 Van Antwerp Bldg.
Mobile, AL 36602
(205) 433-5494/5495

Commerce St., Suite 810
Montgomery, AL 36104
(205) 262-5606

Alaska
3380 C St., Suite 100
Anchorage, AK 99503
(907) 562-0704

Arizona
4428 N. 12th St.
Phoenix, AZ 85014
(602) 264-1721

50 W. Drachman St., Suite 103
Tucson, AZ 85705
(602) 622-7651 (inquiries)
(602) 622-7654 (complaints)

Arkansas
1415 S. University Ave.
Little Rock, AR 72204
(501) 664-7274

California
705—18th St.
Bakersfield, CA 93301
(805) 322-2074

P.O. Box 970
Colton, CA 92324
(714) 825-7280

6101 Ball Rd., Suite 309
Cypress, CA 90630
(714) 527-0680

5070 N. Sixth, Suite 176

Fresno, CA 93710
(209) 222-8111

510—16th St., Suite 550
Oakland, CA 94612
(415) 839-5900

400 S St.
Sacramento, CA 95814
(916) 443-6843

525 B St., Suite 301
San Diego, CA 92101-4408
(619) 234-0966

33 New Montgomery St. Tower
San Francisco, CA 94105
(415) 243-9999

1505 Meridian Ave.
San Jose, CA 95125
(408) 978-8700

P.O. Box 294
San Mateo, CA 94401
(415) 347-1251

P.O. Box 746
Santa Barbara, CA 93102
(805) 963-8657

1111 North Center St.
Stockton, CA 95202
(209) 948-4880/4881

Colorado
P.O. Box 7970
Colorado Springs, CO 80933
(719) 636-1155

1780 S. Bellaire, Suite 700
Denver, CO 80222
(303) 758-2100 (inquiries)
(303) 758-2212 (complaints)

1730 S. College Ave., #303
Fort Collins, CO 80525
(303) 484-1348

432 Broadway
Pueblo, CO 81004
(719) 542-6464

Connecticut

2345 Black Rock Tpk.
Fairfield, CT 06430
(203) 374-6161

2080 Silas Deane Hwy.
Rocky Hill, CT 06067-2311
(203) 529-3575

100 S. Turnpike Rd.
Wallingford, CT 06492
(203) 269-2700 (inquiries)
(203) 269-4457 (complaints)

Delaware

P.O. Box 300
Milford, DE 19963
(302) 422-6300 (Kent)
(302) 856-6969 (Sussex)

P.O. Box 5361
Wilmington, DE 19808
(302) 996-9200

District of Columbia

1012 14th St. NW
Washington, DC 20005
(202) 393-8000

Florida

13770—58th St. N., #309
Clearwater, FL 33520
(813) 535-5522

2976-E Cleveland Ave.
Fort Myers, FL 33901
(813) 334-7331/7152
(813) 597-1322 (Naples)
(813) 743-2279 (Port Charlotte)

3100 University Blvd. S., #23
Jacksonville, FL 32216
(904) 721-2288

2605 Maitland Center Pkwy.
Maitland, FL 32751-7147
(407) 660-9500

16291 NW 57th Ave.
Miami, FL 33014-6709
(305) 625-0307 (inquiries for
   Dade County)
(305) 625-1302 (complaints for
   Dade County)
(305) 524-2803 (inquiries for
   Broward County)
(305) 527-1643 (complaints for
   Broward County)

250 School Rd., Suite 11-W
New Port Richey, FL 34652
(813) 842-5459

P.O. Box 1511
Pensacola, FL 32597-1511
(904) 433-6111

1950 Port St. Lucie Blvd., #211
Port St. Lucie, FL 34952
(407) 878-2010/337-2083

1111 N. Westshore Blvd., Suite
   207
Tampa, FL 33607
(813) 875-6200

2247 Palm Beach Lakes Blvd.,
   #211
West Palm Beach, FL
   33409-3408
(407) 686-2200

Georgia

1319-B Dawson Road
Albany, GA 31707
(912) 883-0744

100 Edgewood Ave., Suite 1012
Atlanta, GA 30303
(404) 688-4910

P.O. Box 2085
Augusta, GA 30903
(404) 722-1574

P.O. Box 2587
Columbus, GA 31902
(404) 324-0712 (inquiries)
(404) 324-0713 (complaints)

6606 Abercorn St., Suite 108-C
Savannah, GA 31416
(912) 354-7521

Hawaii

1600 Kapiolani Blvd., Suite 704
Honolulu, HI 96814
(808) 942-2355

Idaho

409 W. Jefferson
Boise, ID 83702
(208) 342-4649
(208) 467-5547

545 Shoup, Suite 210
Idaho Falls, ID 83402
(208) 523-9754

Illinois

211 W. Wacker Dr.
Chicago, IL 60606
(312) 444-1188 (inquiries)
(312) 346-3313 (complaints)

109 S.W. Jefferson St., #305
Peoria, IL 61602
(309) 673-5194

515 N. Court St.
Rockford, IL 61110
(815) 963-BBB2

Indiana

P.O. Box 405
Elkhart, IN 46515
(219) 262-8996

119 S.E. Fourth St.
Evansville, IN 47708
(812) 422-6879

1203 Webster St.
Fort Wayne, IN 46802
(219) 423-4433

4231 Cleveland St.
Gary, IN 46408
(219) 980-1511/
769-8053/926-5669

Victoria Centre
22 East Washington St.
Indianapolis, IN 46204
(317) 637-0197

320 S. Washington St., #101
Marion, IN 46952
(317) 668-8954/8955

Whitinger Building, Room 150
Muncie, IN 47306
(317) 285-5668

509—85 U.S. #33 North
South Bend, IN 46637
(219) 277-9121

Iowa

2435 Kimberly Road, #110
   North
Bettendorf, IA 52722
(319) 355-6344

1500 Second Avenue SE, #212
Cedar Rapids, IA 52403
(319) 366-5401

615 Insurance Exchange Bldg.
Des Moines, IA 50309
(515) 243-8137

318 Badgerow Bldg.
Siouxland, IA 51101
(712) 252-4501

Kansas

501 Jefferson, Suite 24
Topeka, KS 66607
(913) 232-0455

300 Kaufman Bldg.
Wichita, KS 67202
(316) 263-3146

Kentucky

154 Patchen Dr., Suite 90
Lexington, KY 40502
(606) 268-4128

844 Fourth St.
Louisville, KY 40203
(502) 583-6546

Louisiana

1605 Murray St., Suite 117
Alexandria, LA 71301
(318) 473-4494

2055 Wooddale Blvd.
Baton Rouge, LA 70806
(504) 926-3010

300 Bond St.
Houma, LA 70361
(504) 868-3456

P.O. Box 30297
Lafayette, LA 70593
(318) 234-8341

P.O. Box 1681
Lake Charles, LA 70602
(318) 433-1633

141 De Siard St., Suite 300
Monroe, LA 71201
(318) 387-4600/4601

1539 Jackson Ave.
New Orleans, LA 70130
(504) 581-6222

1401 N. Market St.
Shreveport, LA 71101
(318) 221-8352

Maine

812 Stevens Ave.
Portland, ME 04103
(207) 878-2715

Maryland

2100 Huntingdon Ave.
Baltimore, MD 21211-3215
(301) 347-3990

Massachusetts

Eight Winter St.
Boston, MA 02108
(617) 482-9151 (inquiries)
(617) 482-9190 (complaints)

One Kendall St., Suite 307
Framingham, MA 01701
(508) 872-5585

78 North St., Suite 1
Hyannis, MA 02601
(508) 771-3022

316 Essex St.
Lawrence, MA 01840
(508) 687-7666

106 State Rd., Suite 4
North Dartmouth, MA 02747
(508) 999-6060

293 Bridge St., Suite 324
Springfield, MA 01103
(413) 734-3114

P.O. Box 379
Worcester, MA 01601
(508) 755-2548

Michigan

150 Michigan Ave.
Detroit, MI 48226
(313) 962-7566 (inquiries)
(313) 962-6785 (complaints)

620 Trust Bldg.
Grand Rapids, MI 49503
(616) 774-8236

Minnesota

1745 University Ave.
St. Paul, MN 55104
(612) 646-7700

Mississippi

2917 W. Beach Blvd., #103
Biloxi, MS 39531
(601) 374-2222

105 Fifth St.
Columbus, MS 39701
(601) 327-8594

P.O. Box 390
Jackson, MS 39205-0390
(601) 948-8222

Missouri

306 E. 12th St., Suite 1024
Kansas City, MO 64106
(816) 421-7800

5100 Oakland, Suite 200
St. Louis, MO 63110
(314) 531-3300

205 Park Central East, #509
Springfield, MO 65806
(417) 862-9231

Nebraska

719 N. 48th St.
Lincoln, NE 68504
(402) 467-5261

1613 Farnam St.
Omaha, NE 68102
(402) 346-3033

Nevada

1022 E. Sahara Ave.
Las Vegas, NV 89104
(702) 735-6900/1969

P.O. Box 21269
Reno, NV 89505
(702) 322-0657

New Hampshire

410 S. Main St.
Concord, NH 03301
(603) 224-1991
(800) 852-3757 (toll free in
   NH)

New Jersey

34 Park Pl.
Newark, NJ 07102
(201) 642-INFO

Two Forest Ave.
Paramus, NJ 07652
(201) 845-4044

1721 Rte. #37 East
Toms River, NJ 08753
(201) 270-5577

1700 Whitehorse—Hamilton
Square Rd., Suite D5
Trenton, NJ 08690
(609) 588-0808 (Mercer
County)
(201) 536-6306 (Monmouth
County)
(201) 329-6855 (Middlesex,
Somerset, and Hunterdon
counties)

New Mexico

4600-A Montgomery NE, #200
Albuquerque, NM 87109
(505) 884-0500
(800) 445-1461 (toll free in
NM)

308 N. Locke
Farmington, NM 87401
(505) 326-6501

2407 W. Picacho, Suite B-2
Las Cruces, NM 88005
(505) 524-3130

1210 Luisa St., Suite 5
Santa Fe, NM 87502
(505) 988-3648

New York

346 Delaware Ave.
Buffalo, NY 14202
(716) 856-7180

266 Main St.
Farmingdale, NY 11735
(516) 420-0500

257 Park Ave. South
New York, NY 10010
(212) 533-6200

1122 Sibley Tower
Rochester, NY 14604
(716) 546-6776

100 University Bldg.
Syracuse, NY 13202
(315) 479-6635

120 E. Main St.
Wappinger Falls, NY 12590
(914) 297-6550

30 Glenn St.
White Plains, NY 10603
(914) 428-1230/1231

North Carolina

801 BBB&T Bldg.
Asheville, NC 28801
(704) 253-2392

1130 E. 3rd St., Suite 400
Charlotte, NC 28204
(704) 332-7151
(800) 532-0477 (toll free in
NC)

3608 W. Friendly Ave.
Greensboro, NC 27410
(919) 852-4240/4241/4242

P.O. Box 1882
Hickory, NC 28603
(704) 464-0372

3120 Poplarwood Dr., Suite
101
Raleigh, NC 27604-1080
(919) 872-9240

2110 Cloverdale Ave., #2-B
Winston-Salem, NC 27103
(919) 725-8348

Ohio

P.O. Box 80596
Akron, OH 44308
(216) 253-4590

1434 Cleveland Ave. NW
Canton, OH 44703
(216) 454-9401

898 Walnut St.
Cincinnati, OH 45202
(513) 421-3015

2217 E. 9th St., Suite 200
Cleveland, OH 44115
(216) 241-7678

527 S. High St.
Columbus, OH 43215
(614) 221-6336

40 W. Fourth St., Suite 280
Dayton, OH 45402
(513) 222-5825
(800) 521-8357 (toll free in
    OH)

P.O. Box 269
Lima, OH 45802
(419) 223-7010

P.O. Box 1706
Mansfield, OH 44910
(419) 522-1700

425 Jefferson Ave., Suite 909
Toledo, OH 43604
(419) 241-6276

345 N. Market
Wooster, OH 44691
(216) 263-6444

P.O. Box 1495
Youngstown, OH 44501
(216) 744-3111

Oklahoma

17 S. Dewey
Oklahoma City, OK 73102
(405) 239-6860 (inquiries)
(405) 239-6081 (inquiries)
(405) 239-6083 (complaints)

6711 S. Yale, Suite 230
Tulsa, OK 71436
(918) 492-1266

Oregon

601 S.W. Alder St., Suite 615
Portland, OR 97205
(503) 226-3981

Pennsylvania

528 N. New St.
Bethlehem, PA 18018
(215) 866-8780

6 Marion Court
Lancaster, PA 17602
(717) 291-1151
(717) 232-2800 (Harrisburg)
(717) 846-2700 (York County)

P.O. Box 2297
Philadelphia, PA 19103
(215) 496-1000

610 Smithfield St.
Pittsburgh, PA 15222
(412) 456-2700

P.O. Box 993
Scranton, PA 18501
(717) 342-9129

Puerto Rico

G.P.O. Box 70212
San Juan, PR 00936
(809) 756-5400

Rhode Island

Bureau Park
P.O. Box 1300
Warwick, RI 02887-1300
(401) 785-1212 (inquiries)
(401) 785-1213 (complaints)

South Carolina

1830 Bull St.
Columbia, SC 29201
(803) 254-2525

311 Pettigru St.
Greenville, SC 29601
(803) 242-5052

P.O. Box 8603
Myrtle Beach, SC 29578-8603
(803) 448-6100

Tennessee

P.O. Box 1176 TCAS
Blountville, TN 37617
(615) 323-6311

1010 Market St., Suite 200
Chattanooga, TN 37402
(615) 266-6144
(615) 479-6096 (Bradley
  County)
(615) 266-6144 (Whitfield and
  Murray counties)

P.O. 10327
Knoxville, TN 37939-0327
(615) 522-2552/2130/2139

P.O. Box 41406
Memphis, TN 38174-1406
(901) 272-9641

One Commerce Pl., Suite 1830
Nashville, TN 37239
(615) 254-5872

Texas

3300 S. 14th St., Suite 307
Abilene, TX 79605
(915) 691-1533

P.O. Box 1905
Amarillo, TX 79106
(806) 358-6222

1005 American Plaza
Austin, TX 78701
(512) 476-1616

P.O. Box 2988
Beaumont, TX 77704
(409) 835-5348

202 Varisco Bldg.
Bryan, TX 77801
(409) 823-8148/8149

4535 S. Padre Island Dr.
Corpus Christi, TX 78411
(512) 854-2892

2001 Bryan St., Suite 850
Dallas, TX 75201
(214) 220-2000

1910 East Yandell
El Paso, TX 79903
(915) 545-1212/1264

106 West Fifth St.
Fort Worth, TX 76102
(817) 332-7585

2707 N. Loop West, Suite 900
Houston, TX 77008
(713) 868-9500

P.O. Box 1178
Lubbock, TX 79401
(806) 763-0459

P.O. Box 60206
Midland, TX 79711
(915) 563-1880
(800) 592-4433 (toll free in TX)

P.O. Box 3366
San Angelo, TX 76902
(915) 653-2318

1800 Northeast Loop 410, #400
San Antonio, TX 78217
(512) 828-9441

P.O. Box 6652
Tyler, TX 75711-6652
(214) 581-5704

P.O. Box 7203
Waco, TX 76714-7203
(817) 772-7530

P.O. Box 69
Weslaco, TX 78596
(512) 968-3678

1106 Brook Ave.
Wichita Falls, TX 76301
(817) 723-5526

Utah

385 24th St., Suite 717
Ogden, UT 84401
(801) 399-4701

1588 S. Main
Salt Lake City, UT 84115
(801) 487-4656
(801) 377-2611 (Provo)

Virginia

3608 Tidewater Dr.
Norfolk, VA 23509
(804) 627-5651

701 E. Franklin, Suite 712
Richmond, VA 23219
(804) 648-0016

121 W. Campbell Ave. SW
Roanoke, VA 24011
(703) 342-3455

Washington

127 W. Canal Dr.
Kennewick, WA 99336
(509) 582-0222

2200 Sixth Ave., Suite 828
Seattle, WA 98121-1857
(206) 448-8888

S. 176 Stevens St.
Spokane, WA 99204
(509) 747-1155

P.O. Box 1274
Tacoma, WA 98401
(206) 383-5561

P.O. Box 1584
Yakima, WA 98907
(509) 248-1326

Wisconsin

740 N. Plankinton Ave.
Milwaukee, WI 53202
(414) 273-1600 (inquiries)
(414) 273-0123 (complaints)

Wyoming

BBB/Idaho Falls (Lincoln Park
    and Teton counties)
(208) 523-9754

BBB/Fort Collins (all other
    Wyoming counties)
(800) 873-3222 (toll free)

BANKING RESOURCES

STATE BANKING AUTHORITIES

State banking authorities make and enforce the rules that govern state-chartered banks. Most do not handle complaints against finance companies or retail store creditors, but some do. Many will answer basic questions about banking and credit laws, and, if they cannot handle your complaint, will refer you to an agency that can.

If you have a complaint about the way you were treated by a bank, file it with your state's banking authority. Complaints filed with these agencies typically include those about discrimination, illegal rates of interest, and failure to make required disclosures. The information in this appendix is excerpted from the 1990 edition of the *Consumer's Resource Handbook,* published by the U.S. Office of Consumer Affairs.

Alabama

Superintendent of Banks
166 Commerce St., 3rd Floor
Montgomery, AL 36130
(205) 261-3452

Alaska

Director of Banking and
  Securities
Pouch D
Juneau, AK 99811
(907) 465-2521

Arizona

Superintendent of Banks
3225 N. Central, Suite 815
Phoenix, AZ 85012
(602) 255-4421

Arkansas

Bank Commissioner
323 Center St., Suite 500
Little Rock, AR 72201
(501) 371-1117

California

Superintendent of Banks
235 Montgomery St., Suite 750
San Francisco, CA 94104
(415) 557-3535

Colorado

State Bank Commissioner
First West Plaza, Suite 700
303 W. Colfax
Denver, CO 80204
(303) 866-3131

Connecticut

Banking Commissioner
44 Capitol Ave.
Hartford, CT 06106
(203) 566-4560

Delaware

State Bank Commissioner
P.O. Box 1401
Dover, DE 19903
(302) 736-4235

District of Columbia

Superintendent of Banking and
    Financial Institutions
1350 Pennsylvania Ave. NW.,
    Room 401
Washington, DC 20004
(202) 727-6365

Florida

State Comptroller
State Capitol Bldg.
Tallahassee, FL 32399
(904) 488-0370

Georgia

Commissioner of Banking and
    Finance
2990 Brandywine Rd., Suite
    200
Atlanta, GA 30341
(404) 393-7330

Hawaii

Bank Examiner
P.O. Box 541
Honolulu, HI 96809
(808) 548-7505

Idaho

Director, Department of
    Finance
700 W. State St., 2nd Floor
Boise, ID 83720
(208) 334-3319

Illinois

Commissioner of Banks and
    Trust Companies
119 S. 5th St., Room 400
Springfield, IL 62701
(217) 785-2837

Indiana

Director, Department of
    Financial Institutions
Indiana State Office Bldg.,
    Room 1024
Indianapolis, IN 46204
(317) 232-3955

Iowa

Superintendent of Banking
200 E. Grand, Suite 300
Des Moines, IA 50309
(515) 281-4014

Kansas

State Bank Commissioner
700 Jackson St., Suite 300
Topeka, KS 66603
(913) 296-2266

Kentucky

Commissioner of Banking and
    Securities
911 Leawood Dr.
Frankfort, KY 40601
(502) 564-3390

Louisiana

Commissioner of Financial
    Institutions
P.O. Box 94095
Baton Rouge, LA 70804
(504) 925-4660

Maine

Superintendent of Banking
State House Station, #36
Augusta, ME 04333
(207) 289-3231

Maryland

Bank Commissioner
34 Market Pl.
Baltimore, MD 21202
(301) 333-6262

Massachusetts

Commissioner of Banks
100 Cambridge St.
Boston, MA 02202
(617) 727-3120

Michigan

Commissioner, Financial
    Institutions Bureau
P.O. Box 30224
Lansing, MI 48909
(517) 373-3460

Minnesota

Deputy Commissioner of
    Commerce
500 Metro Square Bldg., 5th
    Floor
St. Paul, MN 55101
(612) 296-2135

Mississippi

Commissioner, Department of
    Banking and Consumer
    Finance
P.O. Box 731
Jackson, MS 39205
(601) 359-1031

Missouri

Commissioner of Finance
P.O. Box 716
Jefferson City, MO 65102
(314) 751-3397

Montana

Commissioner of Financial
    Institutions
1424—9th Ave.
Helena, MT 59620
(406) 444-2091

Nebraska

Director of Banking and
    Finance
301 Centennial Mall S.
Lincoln, NE 68509
(402) 471-2171

Nevada

Commissioner of Financial
  Institutions
406 E. 2nd St.
Carson City, NV 89710
(702) 885-4260

New Hampshire

Bank Commissioner
45 S. Main St.
Concord, NH 03301
(603) 271-3561

New Jersey

Commissioner of Banking
36 W. State St.
Trenton, NJ 08625
(609) 292-3420

New Mexico

Director, Financial Institutions
  Division
Bataan Memorial Bldg., Room
  137
Santa Fe, NM 87503
(505) 827-7740

New York

Superintendent of Banks
2 Rector St.
New York, NY 10006
(212) 618-6642

North Carolina

Commissioner of Banks
P.O. Box 29512
Raleigh, NC 27626
(919) 733-3016

North Dakota

Commissioner of Banking and
  Financial Institutions
State Capitol, Room 1301
Bismarck, ND 58505
(701) 224-2256

Ohio

Superintendent of Banks
2 Nationwide Plaza
Columbus, OH 43215
(614) 466-2932

Oklahoma

Bank Commissioner
Malco Bldg.
4100 N. Lincoln Blvd.
Oklahoma City, OK 73105
(405) 521-2783

Oregon

Deputy Administrator,
  Financial Institutions
  Division
280 Court St. NE
Salem, OR 97310
(503) 378-4140

Pennsylvania

Secretary of Banking
333 Market St., 16th Floor
Harrisburg, PA 17101
(717) 787-6991

Puerto Rico

Commissioner of Banking
P.O. Box S4515
San Juan, PR 00905
(809) 721-5242

Rhode Island

Assistant Director, Banking
  and Securities
100 N. Main St.
Providence, RI 02903
(401) 277-2405

South Carolina

Commissioner of Banking
1026 Sumter St., Room 217
Columbia, SC 29201
(803) 734-1050

South Dakota

Director of Banking and
Finance
State Capitol Bldg.
Pierre, SD 57501
(605) 773-2236

Tennessee

Commissioner of Financial
Institutions
John Sevier Bldg., 4th Floor
Nashville, TN 37219
(615) 741-2236

Texas

Banking Commissioner
2601 N. Lamar
Austin, TX 78705
(512) 479-1200

Utah

Commissioner of Financial
Institutions
P.O. Box 89
Salt Lake City, UT 84110
(801) 530-6502

Vermont

Commissioner of Banking and
Insurance
State Office Bldg.
Montpelier, VT 05602
(802) 828-3301

Virgin Islands

Chair, Banking Board
Kongens Garden, #18
P.O. Box 450
St. Thomas, VI 00801
(809) 774-2991

Virginia

Commissioner of Financial
Institutions
P.O. Box 2-AE
Richmond, VA 23205
(804) 786-3657

Washington

Supervisor of Banking
General Administration Bldg.,
Room 219
Olympia, WA 98504
(206) 753-6520

West Virginia

Deputy Commissioner of
Banking
State Office Bldg. 3, Suite 311
Charleston, WV 25305
(304) 348-2294

Wisconsin

Commissioner of Banking
P.O. Box 7876
Madison, WI 53707
(608) 266-1621

Wyoming

State Examiner
Herschler Bldg., 4th Floor
Cheyenne, WY 82002
(307) 777-6600

FEDERAL TRADE COMMISSION

Contact the Federal Trade Commission (FTC) to file a complaint of federal credit law violation by a mortgage banker, finance company, or any other nonbank creditor. The FTC has 10 regional offices, listed below. Call the one nearest you for instructions on how to file a complaint. Complaints filed with the FTC typically involve failure by a lender to make required disclosures, discrimination, and illegal terms in a credit contract, such as a waiver of consumers' rights. The FTC also publishes free pamphlets (in Spanish and English) on the credit laws it enforces.

The FTC investigates appropriate complaints and imposes fines, but these fines are not used to compensate the aggrieved consumers. When a settlement can't be reached, the FTC can sue. For more information about the FTC, see Chapter 6.

FTC National Headquarters
6th and Pennsylvania Aves. NW
Washington, DC 20580
(202) 326-2222

FTC Regional Offices
1718 Peachtree St. NW
Atlanta, GA 30367
(405) 347-4836

10 Causeway St.
Boston, MA 02222
(617) 565-7240

55 E. Monroe St.
Chicago, IL 60603
(312) 353-4423

118 St. Clair Ave.
Cleveland, OH 44114
(216) 522-4210

8303 Elmbrook Dr.
Dallas, TX 75247
(214) 767-7050

1405 Curtis St.
Denver, CO 80202
(303) 844-2271

11000 Wilshire Blvd.
Los Angeles, CA 90024
(213) 209-7890

26 Federal Plaza
New York, NY 10278
(212) 264-1207

901 Market St.
San Francisco, CA 94103
(415) 995-5220

915 Second Ave.
Seattle, WA 98174
(206) 442-4655

FEDERAL RESERVE OFFICES

Your regional Federal Reserve Bank accepts complaints of federal credit law violations by any bank or other financial institution. It refers these complaints within 15 days to the appropriate agency. Although the Federal Reserve Bank's jurisdiction is limited to state-chartered banks that are members of the Federal Reserve System, its enforcement powers extend beyond these institutions, and it can deal with all complaints. Following are the addresses and telephone numbers of the Federal Reserve Bank's national headquarters and its regional offices.

Federal Reserve National Headquarters

Board of Governors of the
Federal Reserve System
20th and C Sts. NW
Washington, DC 20551
(202) 452-3000

Federal Reserve Regional Offices

104 Marietta St. NW
Atlanta, GA 30303
(404) 521-8500

600 Atlantic Ave.
Boston, MA 02106
(617) 973-3000

230 S. LaSalle St.
Chicago, IL 60690
(312) 322-5322

1455 E. Sixth St.
Cleveland, OH 44114
(216) 579-2000

400 S. Akard St.
Dallas, TX 75202
(214) 651-6111

925 Grand Ave.
Kansas City, MO 64198
(816) 881-2000

250 Marquette Ave.
Minneapolis, MN 55480
(612) 340-2345

33 Liberty St.
New York, NY 10045
(212) 720-5000

10 Independence Mall
Philadelphia, PA 19106
(215) 574-6000

701 E. Byrd St.
Richmond, VA 23219
(804) 697-8000

101 Market St.
San Francisco, CA 94105
(415) 974-2000

411 Locust St.
St. Louis, MO 63102
(314) 444-8444

HUD OFFICES

The Department of Housing and Urban Development (HUD) is the federal agency responsible for administering federal programs related to the nation's housing needs. HUD is divided into two sections: the Office of Fair Housing and Equal Opportunity and the Office of Neighborhoods, Voluntary Associations and Consumer Protection. The Office of Fair Housing is chiefly concerned with the housing problems of lower-income and minority groups. The Office of Neighborhoods protects consumer interests in all housing and community development activities. For information, publications, advice, and referrals, or to file complaints about local housing practices, contact the regional office nearest you.

National Headquarters

451 Seventh St. SW
Washington, DC 20410
(202) 755-5111

Regional Offices

10 Causeway St., Room 375
Boston, MA 02222
(617) 565-5234

26 Federal Plaza
New York, NY 10278
(212) 264-8053

105 S. Seventh St.
Philadelphia, PA 19106
(215) 597-2560

75 Spring St. SW
Atlanta, GA 30303
(404) 331-5136

626 W. Jackson Blvd.
Chicago, IL 60606
(312) 353-5680

1600 Throckmorton
Fort Worth, TX 76113
(817) 885-5401

1103 Grand Ave.
Kansas City, MO 64106
(816) 374-6432

1405 Curtis St.
Denver, CO 80202
(303) 844-4513

450 Golden Gate Ave.
San Francisco, CA 94102
(415) 556-4752

1321 Second Ave.
Seattle, WA 98101
(206) 442-5414

GLOSSARY

The following defines terms used throughout this manual. Italicized terms are defined in other entries of this glossary.

Acceleration   The process by which a lender, such as a bank, makes the entire amount of a loan due and requests that it be paid at once. Usually triggered by the borrower's *default*.

Acceptance   Agreement to a contract *offer* on the terms presented. An acceptance can be verbal, written, or an action, such as the payment of money. Once accepted, a contract is created.

Accounts receivable   Money that is owed.

Agent   Someone who acts on behalf of another.

Amortization schedule   A schedule of equal payments over a specified period to pay off both a debt and the *interest* on that debt. This is provided by a lender, such as a bank, when someone takes out a loan.

Annual percentage rate (APR)   The *interest* for each year of a loan, expressed as a percentage of the money borrowed.

Arbitration   Method of settling disputes in which the two sides submit arguments to a neutral third party or panel that makes a decision after listening to both sides and considering the evidence.

Assignee   The person to whom a right or interest is given or transferred.

Assignment   Formally giving someone a right or obligation.

Attorney in fact   The person designated in a power of attorney to handle the affairs of the person making the power of attorney.

Bankruptcy   A procedure rescheduling or canceling a person's debts. Typically, a court seizes all of a person's assets and disburses them among creditors. A small amount, an "exemption," is reserved by the court for the individual—once the individual has been officially discharged of all debts. Under some forms of bankruptcy, the individual must pay back a percentage of those debts afterward, as decided by the court.

Bond   A monetary guarantee that should a contractor fail to perform a contract fully, compensation will be awarded up to the bond's limit.

Breach   Reason for suing based on failure to live up to a legally binding promise.

Clear and conspicuous   A phrase used to describe how the important parts of a lending contract must appear so that the borrower will notice them, as required by the *Truth in Lending Act*. The costs of credit (for purposes of comparison), as well as the loan's significant benefits, obligations, and restrictions, must all be "clear and conspicuous" on the contract.

Collateral   Something of value provisionally given to the lender during the life of the loan. In the event of a default, it can be seized and sold by the lender.

Collection   A method of obtaining debts owed.

Confession of judgment   A clause that allows the lender to appoint a lawyer on the borrower's behalf in order to get a court *judgment* on a debt without notifying the borrower. The Credit Practices Rule makes this provision illegal in consumer loans.

Conflict of laws   The body of laws a court uses to decide whether its own previous rulings or those of some other court related to the case are to be used in a specific case.

Conservator   A person or corporation appointed by a court to handle the affairs or property of another who is unable to do so because of *incapacity* or being under the age of majority.

Consideration   Something of value each side gives up in order to make a contract valid. Usually in the form of money-for-goods, this may also be a promise or service.

Conveyance   An exchange of two things, usually used when referring to land transactions.

Cosigner   One who adds his or her signature to the loan of another and thereby assumes equal responsibility for payments on that loan.

Counteroffer   An invitation to exchange promises and enter into a contract, thereby canceling an earlier *offer* by the other side in the prospective contract. The counteroffer must be accepted to make a contract.

Credit bureau A company that maintains records of consumers' credit histories for potential creditors who pay a fee for a report.

Credit history A history of credits used, loans paid, and outstanding debts owed by an individual.

Credit report A document that shows all or part of a person's *credit history.*

Creditworthiness An evaluation of whether a person should be granted a loan or a line of credit, made at the discretion of the bank or other lender organization.

Damages Amount of money or other relief requested by a plaintiff in a lawsuit.

Default Declaration by a lender that a borrower has failed to make scheduled payments on a loan, thereby enabling the lender to seize the property or other *collateral.*

Disclosures Affirmative statement made to ensure certain information is communicated. Lenders are required by the *Truth in Lending Act* to make certain disclosures to their customers.

Discount rate The *interest* rate charged by the *Federal Reserve Board* to its member banks.

Duress Unlawful pressure on a person to do something she or he would not voluntarily do. A contract shown to have been made under duress will be declared invalid.

Excused counterperformance A *remedy* for a broken contract whereby, if one side fails to live up to its side of the agreement, the other may not be obligated to live up to its side.

Federal Reserve Board A 13-member board appointed by the president and approved by Congress. It regulates both banks in the United States and the entire U.S. monetary system. (Complaints about banks that are members of the Federal Reserve System should be made here.)

Federal Trade Commission A commission appointed by the president responsible for regulating trade practices, including those of finance companies. (Problems concerning nonbank loans—e.g., department store credit—should be reported to the FTC.)

Finance charge *Interest* and other added fees, in addition to the cost of goods or services, to be paid when a purchase is made in installments; usually must be stated as an *annual percentage rate.*

Fraud Intentional deception, grounds for canceling a contract. Also a defense to breaching a contract.

Grace period Short period, usually 10 to 15 days after a loan payment is due, during which the borrower will be assessed no late charge or additional interest.

Guardian See *Conservator.*

Housing code State or local regulations that mandate sanitary and technical requirements that must be met before a residence can be occupied.

Implied warranty of habitability The legal obligation of a landlord to provide tenants with livable, safe, and sanitary housing.

Incapacity A declaration by a court that a person is unable to handle his or her own affairs because of a mental or physical condition.

Interest Payment a lender receives for lending money.

Joint tenancy with a right of survivorship Form of ownership in which property is equally shared by all owners and is automatically transferred to the surviving owners if one owner dies.

Judgment Final decision announced or written by a judge about the rights and claims of each side in a lawsuit.

Liquidity The ease with which assets may be converted to cash; the amount of a person's assets in a state of cash or near cash (as in a bank's savings account).

Loan principal The amount of money borrowed, as contrasted with *interest* to be paid on that amount.

Material terms The essential details that define each side's rights and obligations under a contract.

Mechanic's lien Legal claim by a service person to hold or sell property as security for a debt.

Mediation Informal alternative to suing in which both sides to a dispute meet with a neutral third party (mediator) to negotiate a resolution. The resolution is usually put into a written agreement that is signed by both sides.

Negotiable Something that can be exchanged for cash, such as a check or promissory note.

Notary public One who has finished a course of study and is licensed by the state to verify the legitimacy of documents signed in his or her presence.

Notice of default A written notice by one side in an agreement to the second stating that the contract has been *breached* and reclaiming whatever benefits the second party gained by the contract.

Offer An invitation to make a contract or to exchange promises. (See also *Counteroffer.*)

Payable on demand   An item payable within a reasonable time after it is requested (e.g., a note or loan payable on demand may be requested at any time).

Performance   The completion of one side of an agreement or contract; carrying out one's end of a bargain.

Prepayment   A payment before a sum is due.

Prepayment penalty   Charge that penalizes a borrower who pays off a loan earlier than required by the terms of the loan.

Prime rate   *Interest* banks charge their best customers.

Quasi-contract   A court award of money for work already done before the contract was broken. A *remedy* for *breach* of contract.

Quiet enjoyment   A common-law requirement that landlords who rent residences guarantee peace and quiet to tenants.

Receivership proceedings   A court action during which either money or property of one party is put under the control of an outside, responsible party, called a receiver.

Release   A legal document that relieves someone of an obligation or potential obligation.

Remedy   The means by which someone is compensated for an injury. Types of remedies include restitution, *damages,* and *specific performance.* Also, a penalty to prevent the breaking of a contract.

Revocable trust   Property held by one party for the sake and benefit of a second but that can be taken back by the second party.

Sublease   Rental of a rented tenancy to a third party, in effect turning the first renter into a landlord. The original renter remains liable to the original landlord for the terms of the lease.

Secured loan   A loan in which the lender holds an interest in property of the borrower to assure that the loan will be paid.

Security interest   Rights a creditor has to a borrower's *collateral* if the borrower *defaults* on a loan.

Specific performance   Equitable *remedy* in which a court requires a party to do something. For example, a judge may order that a one-of-a-kind object be returned to its original owner.

Statute of frauds   State law that specifies what contracts must be in writing to be considered legal and enforceable.

Substantial performance   Completion of a project sufficiently to warrant payment for all service, less the amount not completed.

Successors   Persons who take over the rights, responsibilities, or property of another.

Truth in Lending Act   Federal law that requires certain disclosures to be made to all those who apply for a loan.

Unconscionability   An unreasonable and challengeable provision in a contract that results from unequal bargaining power between the parties, such as when one side is forced by a take-it-or-leave-it proposal to accept the unreasonable provision. A court may strike down the unconscionable clause but uphold the rest of the contract.

Waiver   A purposeful, voluntary surrender of a known right.

Waiver of exemption   A clause in a loan agreement that waives a borrower's legal right to restrict a court's seizure of personal property if the borrower *defaults*.

Warranty   Guarantee by the seller that the condition of what is being transferred is exactly as described.

Writ of attachment   A judge's order to seize persons or property in order to bring them under court control to pay off a court *judgment*.

BIBLIOGRAPHY

$\mathbf{T}$his bibliography of form books and books about general contract law should be used to supplement the resources listed in each part. Some books are written for lawyers and law students, others for nonlawyers. Many include a variety of forms with do-it-yourself instructions.

Form books should be used with some caution. Their sample forms will probably have to be adjusted to your particular situation. In any event, be sure you understand all parts of a sample form before using any of it.

The Complete Legal Kit, by the Consumer Law Foundation. Running Press, 125 S. 22nd St., Philadelphia, PA 19103. (215) 567-5080. 1988. 164 pages. $17.95.
Self-help book with over 150 ready-to-use tear-out forms. Covers employment, leases, credit, assignments, and loans, among other subjects, all in plain language.
Contracts, by Gordon D. Schaber and Claude D. Rohwer. Nutshell Series, West Publishing Co., P.O. Box 43526, St. Paul, MN 55164. (612) 228-2500. 1984. 425 pages. $10.95.
Written for law students by law professors; covers contract theory as it would be taught to first-year students. Complete, easy-to-read (although not in plain language) discussion of all contract theory, but more than you may ever need.
Everyday Legal Forms, by Irving J. Sloan. Oceana Group, 75 Main St., Dobbs Ferry, NY 10522. (914) 693-1320. 1984. 146 pages. $8.50.
Thirty-four legal forms for business agreements, domestic rela-

tions, real estate, estate planning (including wills and trusts), powers of attorney, and promissory notes, among others. Covers protection needed in common legal transactions and background of forms in the book.

How To Avoid Lawyers, by Don Biggs. Garland Press, 136 Madison Ave., New York, NY 10016. (212) 686-7492. 1989. 1,000 pages. $27.95.

Basic reference tool, perfect for do-it-yourselfers. Overview of most everyday law, including real estate, domestic law, and probate, plus hundreds of forms, including powers of attorney and promissory notes.

Instant Legal Forms, by Ralph E. Troisi. Tab Books, Blue Ridge Summit, PA 17294. (717) 794-2191. 1989. 305 pages. $15.95.

Book of easy-to-use forms, including rental agreement, deed, promissory note, home-improvement contract, and living will.

Legal Agreements in Plain English, by Joel D. Joseph and Jeffrey Hiller. Contemporary Books, Inc., 180 N. Michigan Ave., Chicago, IL 60601. (312) 782-9181. 1982. 136 pages. $9.95.

Principles, definitions, and forms for conducting basic legal business. Agreements with simple explanations and tear-out contracts. Includes setting up a business, separation and divorce, loans, wills, home improvements, and buying, renting, or selling a home.

The Legal Forms Kit. Homestead Publishing Co., 4455 Torrance Blvd., Torrance, CA 90503. (213) 214-3559. 1987. 320 pages. $41.95.

Forms for almost every legal topic with plain-language explanations for each. Topics include real estate, credit and collections, employment, loans and debts, small businesses and partnerships, among others.

Make Your Own Contract, by Stephen Elias. Nolo Press, 950 Parker St., Berkeley, CA 94710. (415) 549-1976. 1987. 208 pages. $12.95.

Detailed workbook for writing your own contract in plain language. Includes many variations of forms, plus warnings and tips.

Personal Lawyer. Bloc Publishing Co., 800 S.W. 37th Ave., Suite 765, Coral Gables, FL 33134. (800) 888-2562. 1988. $50.

IBM computer program of five do-it-yourself forms: will, power of attorney, statement of guardianship, promissory note, and lease. Question-and-answer format to complete user's personalized form.

The Power of Attorney Book, by Dennis Clifford. Nolo Press, 950 Parker St., Berkeley, CA 94710. (415) 549-1976. 1988. 280 pages. $17.95.

All forms and instructions to create your own conventional or durable power of attorney as well as advice on when and how to delegate authority over your health and personal affairs.

Sign Here, by Mari W. Privette. Doubleday and Co., 501 Franklin Ave., Garden City, NY 11530. (212) 765-6500. 1985. 297 pages. $9.95. Easy-to-use book that explains contract terms, requirements, and remedies, and includes sample contracts and a complete glossary. In question-and-answer form, includes insurance, marriage and divorce, real estate warranties, and credit.

What You Should Know about Contracts, by Robert A. Farmer. Simon and Schuster, 1230 Ave. of the Americas, New York, NY 10020. (212) 698-7000. 1979 (out of print). 189 pages. $3.95.

Good, clear, plain-language discussion of contract basics, including offer and acceptance, consideration, defenses, and breach of contract. Also sample contracts and short glossary. No longer in bookstores.

About the Authors

George Milko is the Director of Education for HALT. He is the author of *Real Estate,* co-author of *After the Crash: An Information Kit for Victims of Airline Disasters,* and editor of *Alternative Compensation Strategies: Creating No Lawsuit Options to the Tort System.* Mr. Milko received his J.D. in 1983 from the National Law Center at George Washington University. He is a member of the District of Columbia Bar.

Kay Ostberg is the Deputy Director of HALT. She is the author of *Using a Lawyer, Probate, Directory of Lawyers Who Sue Lawyers,* and the "Attorney Discipline National Survey and Report." Ms. Ostberg received her J.D. in 1983 from the National Law Center at George Washington University. She is a member of the National Federation of Paralegal Associations Advisory Board.

Theresa Meehan Rudy is a Program Specialist for HALT. She is the author of *Small Claims Court, Fee Arbitration: Model Rules and Commentary,* and "Arbitrating Lawyer-Client Fee Disputes: A National Survey." Ms. Rudy received her B.A. in 1981 from the University of Massachusetts, Amherst, and is a lay arbitrator for the District of Columbia Bar's fee arbitration program.